A River of Tears—
The River of Hope

by

Orit Murad Rehany &
Aaron Murad

authorHOUSE®

AuthorHouse™ LLC
1663 Liberty Drive
Bloomington, IN 47403
www.authorhouse.com
Phone: 1-800-839-8640

Published by AuthorHouse   03/22/2014

ISBN: 978-1-4918-3492-3 (sc)
ISBN: 978-1-4918-3493-0 (e)

Library of Congress Control Number: 2013922278

Table of Contents

Dedication

I am dedicating this book to my parents Lulu Khatoun and Mordechai Murad.

Acknowledgments

*W*e must explain how we started to write this book that took about three years to complete and which amazingly encompassed the entire family of Rabbi Ezra.

Rabbi Ezra's name is still alive and circulating as one of the greatest personalities and role models that should never be forgotten. Our commitment, in the beginning of this road, was to shed the light that Rabbi Ezra shone for his generation, and bring it over to our generation and accelerate his name to new heights that he deserves.

Thanks to our beloved Uncle Yosef-Haim for leaving us a family tree, that as simple as it may have been, many details were unknown to the younger generation. This 'treasure' enabled us to continue our research, combine it with the history of the time, and end it with the first steps of our settlement in Israel.

We did not think that our collection of handouts were so great, to be called a book. We did not mean to be so diverse, interesting, motivating and compelling. But we think that we did a great job in trying to preserve our legacy and our family's history.

Articles were contributed to this book from family members, who assisted us to produce the stories about our parents and their experiences. We must mention, without Isaac Murad (Rabbi

Ezra's son) article, the picture would not have been painted the same colors. Emile Murad who shared so many beautiful stories that is a pleasure to read, Eli Murad who shared one of the funniest stories, on experiences from the beginning of the 50s. Ruth Aslan who helped achieving our goal. Ora Rejuan contributed much to the success of the book.

Most and foremost Aaron Murad who contributed a chapter to this book, and other insights and experiences of his up bringing in Baghdad. To him we owe thank you and appreciation. Aaron and I have worked closely together to achieve the best results for quality published book that we can be proud of. We are indeed proud to introduce this material for our families and the general public.

We must acknowledge Uncle Isaac and his adorable wife Simcha, for their unsurpassed generousity and guidance that will forever serve as a role model.

I am a firm believer in learning through life stories and experiences and through the wisdom of our sages. Every story has a lesson of inspiration and motivation, therefore, the stories of our ancestors are as alive and classical as many stories of our generation.

I would love to share one of my favorite stories taught in Jewish day schools. It is actually related to the celebration of Tu B'shvat, the holiday of the trees:

"One old man was planting a small tree in his garden. A boy passed by and asked the old man to whom the plant will be, and when it will give its fruit. The old man answered the boy that the plant will start giving its fruit only maybe after ten years. The boy was puzzled and asked the old man, if he thinks that he will live ten years to eat from the fruit of this plant. The old man answered that he is planting it for his children and grandchildren so they can eat from its fruit, just like his ancestors did for him."

The moral of this story is clear and it resonates with our intentions to give the gift of legacy to our families, and to educate the general public.

Like everything else, when you start a project you must anticipate challenges and delays. Our book has had many obstacles along its way, until finally, and by pure accident, we fell into the good hands of our fabulous editor Justin Spizman, a lawyer and a writer. He did a great job in editing this book, and making the process so smooth and enjoyable.

We hope, that you will learn as much wealth of information as we did, that it will inspire and motivate you, to entrench your passion and dedication into your own project.

What did I learn through this process? I am mostly thankful to have finally discovered myself and who I am. That digging into your soul so deeply will eventually produce excellent results.

And to whom I dedicate this book? I dedicate it to my twelve grandchildren. I am thrilled and grateful to have seen my exciting triplet girls Eve Claire Chava, May Lauren Aviva, Lily Kate (Lulu Khatoun) and that Lily's name carries an abundance of history and personalities, all mentioned in this book, Alon, my youngest son, chose to name her after his grandmother Lulu Kahtoun.

To whom is Aaron dedicating this book? He is dedicating it to his four grandchildren which includes the recent birth of his twin grandchildren, a boy and a girl, Tayler Shalv and Sage Lev – which again the name Lev carries an abundance of history, named after Lulu Khatoun.

How lovely is the name Lulu Khatoun, sounds so ancient and mysterious!!

Montreal, June 8, 2013, the celebration of putting on Teffilin
Mordechai Rehany and Zachary Rehany

Montreal June 8, 2013, Bar Mitzvah celebration, family picture of Mordechai
and Rose Rehany with their 6 children

(from left) Eve Claire Chava, May Lauren Aviva, Lily Kate (Lulu Khatoun)

Twins, Taylor (boy) and Sage (girl)

Great Aunt is always a source of inspiration

New Jersey July 2013, celebrating Taylor's Brith and Sage's naming.
Sitting: Orit Murad, Renat Murad. Standing: Morry Murad, Eileen
Murad, Tiqva Murad, Saul Rehany, Aaron Murad

Sweet & Sour Memories

September 10th, just one day before a very sad day in the United States. And I am here pondering and contemplating!!

Should I tell you about my journey, or my legacy? Is it going to change your reality? Is it going to inspire you, make you eager to learn more from my experience and the experiences of my family?

Suddenly, my fear has just changed its outfit and luckily it became the outfit of courage and I opened my pages to read and decided to ask you first: Did you know that I have four nationalities on my shoulders, four cultures, four languages, four ways of life, that each one is very special and unique, each one had taught me another culture and another experience, to lead me to light my bulb to ignite and direct me, to make me feel excited from all the sweet or sour memories, and to unload them forever put on a plate on a picnic table.

We cherish those sweet and sour moments, our nature is to remember. The more we think the more we remember.

Are there only sweet memories? Is there only sour memories? History had taught us that they both intertwine; that those memories have a message, a role model, an experience, a lesson, comfort, hope, inspiration, intimidation, support, imagination. . .

Actually, we were born to overcome and direct our negative forces, we were born with freedom, freedom of choice, and only we are able to control our negative feelings and actions. Those negative feelings, by nature, override the positive emotions, approaches or deeds.

My story touches hearts; my story is about family and sharing, the beauty of family or family values. Those values took me and brought me up to this moment.

Baghdad Iraq, the country where I was born, absorbed my childhood's culture, did not know that one day I have to sweat for myself, took everything for granted, I am at my parents house, surrounded by love, with brothers sister, aunts uncles and cousins, community life existing for 2600 years, proud of my heritage, feel blessed, until events changed that tranquil picture, that all of a sudden the River became A River of Tears. Where are my hopes? Where is the continuation of my life, or community life? Is that all? Do you call this a sad moment in my life? It has just been beautiful, as surreal as the two rivers, what happened to make it change? Why? Is my skin color red? Or did I come from the Moon, or the Jungle?

No, No, No, neither of the above, you were just told to step out, to move, to disappear, or else. . . . And you had to take your one luggage that you were allowed to take and run as far and as fast as you can. Political upheaval, political changes, Anti-Semitism, Natzism and the full practice of hatred.

"So my dear friends, the saga continues and naturally, my next country became **Israel***. The country of my ancestors, my fathers, the country of the Bible, the Promised Land, it is not the country of the devil, of slaughter or gas chambers, pogroms, it is all white and blue it has the peaceful Dove and the Olive branch. It unites us all together, from all corners of the world, wherever we are, it encompasses the Ten Lost Tribes that has just been discovered, you see nothing is lost. Are these the Happy Moments of my life? Are these the moments I have been waiting for?"*

I became a refugee, in my own beautiful country, in the country of Next Year in Jerusalem. . .I lived in transition camps, amongst wild creatures, dangerous creatures, then I had to move up as much as I could take myself up, as far as I could, I threw the ball up, and surprisingly the ball stayed up. . . . Can it be? Yes it could, it all depends on you. Yes, the more we think the more we remember good or bad sweet or sour. We grow, we discover and we learn. Growing up and moving toward the right channels of life, discovering that there is more to discover. Curiosity and discovery are natural beings.

What else is there in the world, how the seas and oceans look like, other continents, lands, countries, cultures, languages. . . .

So, Canada became my next and third country, next destination the next stop. Montreal, where I built my own family, raising my own children, buying my own house, learning another language or two, French and English, to continue work hard, to continue to achieve to broaden my horizon, to progress and succeed, to give our children the best we could under the harsh conditions of the winter. . . Really? Is that what worries you? Was this the happiest time of my life? Over thirty years in Montreal, where another political upheaval occurred, to find out that history repeats itself, that another group of people were unhappy unhappy with their situation, demanding separation, demanding the impossible, can it be? Is it possible? Only future can tell, or the fortune teller.

Yes, there were so many happy occasions along with sweet and sour memories, family get together, friends to socialize with, to gossip about, to brag, to compete or family to fight with, don't take life for granted things can change, enjoy the moment, give up forgive and forget but who am I to say all that? Yet, this can give a bad taste to your coffee, your coffee is stale, and a feeling of ouch again. . . which reminds me of "you cut the Turkey before I arrived"?

Immigrants who came to Montreal mostly to fulfill their dreams, would say to themselves to never give up, there is always a light at the end of the tunnel. Oh yes, beautiful Canadian scenery, beautiful country, beautiful people.

Again, nobody said to leave, but the atmosphere was for leaving, settling somewhere safer with brighter future therefore many young professionals moved to Toronto to start new life. . . .

Fantastic memories, the more you think, the more you can remember. . . .

So what is next? Wasn't it enough? True, my dear friends, this journey has tears of happiness and sadness. Sweet and sour, good and bad, much like the surreal

River of Tears, just like the rapidly flowing water in the River of Tears, the water that feeds the fertile crescent of the land of Abraham.

Yes my dear friends, next comes the best country in the world, **The United States**, where you can experience the full meaning of freedom, the most democratic country on earth with its unlimited possibilities and opportunities that tells you that all depends on you, on your dreams and that the measure of your accomplishments and success is as big as your dream, you could reach the sky or you could stay on earth it is all you. . .do not blame anyone, there is no one to blame, blame yourself only.

Here comes beautiful Florida, beaches, ocean, clear sky, flocks of birds, green trees, actually everywhere is green, you are surrounded by green color which happens to be my husband's favorite color, light green, dark green, bright green, the sun that says to you "you are so lucky to have me" I can change your life, I have the power to make you happy, I hold in my big round hand the secrets of the world, witnessing the creation of God.

When you meet new people in Florida, introduce yourself and the conversation will start and the first question you ask is "Where did you come from? Which is your home town?"

The more you think, the more you can remember. . . . Then you go back to the memories of the surreal *River of Tears*, you go back to your beginning and ask: Was this the journey that I wanted to create? Was this the journey I wanted to travel through? And you think: Does it have good and bad positive or negative or which one is more present in you the sweet or the sour? Then you reach the conclusion that the sour is more present in you but it is your choice to make it sweeter, just the way you were created with free choice. Without free choice who am I? What could I do or not do without my free choice?

This journey of my life has been terribly different, but terribly interesting. It has been hard, but manageable, it has been tough, but it strengthened me, this journey has been with great loss, greater than you could ever imagine, but I gained my losses back, the only loss that I never regained was the loss of my father and brother in Baghdad, the loss of my mother in Montreal and the loss of my brother and sister in Israel, and I am standing here alone just thinking and remembering how it all started, and realized that it all started from the fading **River of Tears to the Rivers of Hope** and how much I desire to share, to unload. . .

And how much I desire to upload wisdom and share information for you to learn. Is there a limit, or a border to learning? Or maybe we create our own borders and limits?

Open your heart to hope
As you follow the journey of
The Saga of Two Torah Scrolls
in A River of Tears The River of hope

And beyond

Introduction

*T*he following pages contain the stories and memories of the Murad family's journey from Iraq to Israel during the early 1950s. This was unique and interesting time both historically and politically, and our family feels it is important to record our experiences for the posterity of our younger generations.

You will find that the book is divided into four chapters, each with its own theme. We start with family to give you background and to establish a familiarity with our lineage. We then move on to history in order to provide an overview of the importance of Iraq and Israel to the Jewish community. Next we take you on our family's journey to the Holy Land, and paint a picture of what it was like to live in such a dynamic time. Finally we recount our experiences once we arrived in the Promised Land, the place the Murad's are proud to call home.

You will find that our book does not follow a traditional structure or plot line, but instead provides individual accounts and personal vignettes of our family's connected legacy. We are striving to present a complete account of this monumental period in order to preserve multiple experiences and perspectives.

Our stories are filled with excitement, adventure, heartache, pain, loss, love and laughter. We are blessed to be able to share our legacy with you, and we hope these stories will be shared for generations to come.

Thank you.

Part I
The Family

Before you can understand our journey, you have to understand our heritage. Our family is a large one, spanning millennia and the entire world. There were Rabbis, scholars, leaders, workers, and anything and everything in between. The pride our family carries through generation-to-generation, acts as the common fabric that ties us all together. Our history is one of which we are very proud, and it grows stronger and more entrenched with each member's accomplishments and success.

Heritage is a concept passed down and inherited with the birth and life of each generation. We view our family as a beautiful portrait, with each family member adding his or her own legacy and brushstrokes to the magnificent piece of art. It is ever changing and as the colors mold together, they become more entrenched and interwoven. We hope you identify with our family's history and recognize how it parallels your own. Family is the cornerstone for our story and as our family grows, so does our wonderful legacy.

To understand the beginning of the Murad family history, we must go back to the 17th century, and we have the honor to introduce to you the people and the stories that shaped our wonderful legacy.

Eliyahu Mordechai, nowadays Eliyahu Murad, was born in Baghdad in 1800, and ultimately became the founder of the Murad dynasty. How can we recover more information about Eliyahu's ancestry or family names? Since Biblical times people's identification was only by the mention of their father and grandfather's names. Therefore, the only source available to us, pertaining to Eliyahu's identity, is that Eliyahu was the son of Joseph (1770), who was the son of Isaac (1740). Isaac, from what we know, was the son of Sasson (1720). This is as far as we can go in retrieving Eliyahu's identity. The reasons we cannot go back further are political changes, turmoil, and wars that were responsible for ruining Baghdad and the Middle East alike, disenabling the preservation of records. This was during the period of the Mongol Empire.

What we know about Eliyahu is based on stories that were passed down by word of mouth and circulated among the community; they told that Eliyahu was a peddler and sold spices in the Arab villages. Reportedly, Eliyahu was born to a distinguished and well-known family, was respected among the community, and was loved by everyone who knew him. He was a righteous, modest, and brave man,who gained well-deserved fame and reverence. He caught the attention of the Chairman of the Jewish Court, the distinguished Rabbi David (or Hakham David, reflection of a great respect) who chose him to marry his only daughter Khatoun.

Mighty floods from the two rivers, Tigris and Euphrates, caused catastrophic epidemics, which lasted seven years, during which most of the Iraqi community fled to the desert to save their lives where they lived amongst dangerous species for years. Rabbi David had another choice, to go back to Persia, to the Capital city of Shushan, where he was born. Rabbi David was joined by his daughter Khatoun and her husband Eliyahu. In Persia, Khatoun was expecting the birth of her first born, and while there, Khatoun and

Eliyahu visited the tomb of Mordechai and Queen Esther from the story recorded in the book of Esther in the Bible. Being so excited and inspired from the sight of the tomb, they vowed to name their newborn Mordechai.

On one of his business trips to sell spices, Eliyahu never returned home. Although details are limited, it is assumed that Arabs assassinated him. After Eliyahu's tragic and untimely death at the young age of fifty, stories would still be told about his righteousness and modesty, and eventually his memory was inscribed, by his great grandchildren, in one of the two surviving Torah Scrolls from Baghdad. Our family history continues with the short life of Mordechai Murad.

Mordechai Murad, the eldest son of Khatoun and Eliyahu was born in 1827-1877 in Persia. When he approached the young age of marriage he wed the daughter of the British Consul in Persia, Mazal Gabbai, the future mother of Rabbi Ezra. Unfortunately, Mordechai's life was short and he died at the age of fifty from unknown causes. His wife Mazal, was an educated woman for her generation, and was blessed with longer life than her husband. The widowed status of Mazal, along with her eight children consisting of four boys and four girls, compelled her to go back to her father's house, the notable and respected Rabbi David. The children, growing up at their grandfather's house, were often identified by the name of Rabbi (Or Hackam) David, rather than their original name Murad.

Hackam David Papu acted as Hackam Bashi (Chief Rabbi) in the 18th century during the rule of the Turkish Empire. The following story sheds light on David's personality, righteousness and his ability to judge.

"One of the complaint cases that came to the attention of Rabbi David was from a neighbor living in a house right beside the house of the Head of the Community. The neighbor's bedroom window was facing the Head of the Community's window which obviously made it easy to look inside the room.

Rabbi David solved this case by ordering the Head of the community to close his window completely!!

"Let Rabbi David go back to Persia, where he came from" said the Head of the community in his anger.

Rabbi David heard, did not hesitate, took this matter seriously, sold his house in a haste and was planning to leave for his journey to Persia the day after Shabatt.

The news about Rabbi David's decision traveled fast to the attention of the Head of the Community, when Rabbi David was absent from Seuda Shlishit (The third meal on Shabatt evening), which always took place in his house every Saturday evening.

Over and over again, the Head of the Community tried to persuade Rabbi David to change his mind and stay."

1. How would you have solved this case?

2. What did you learn from this story?

Hackam David Papu in center wearing black

A Rich Heritage:
The Children of Mordechai and Mazal Murad

Chahla Murad (1850-1937) Chahla dedicated her life to social work and helping people in need. Society was much different during Chahla's lifetime than it is today. She was divorced, which was a rare and tragic blemish for a woman in her generation. It meant she was unable to ever marry again. Yet, Chahla did not allow her personal life to interfere with her public life. After her divorce, she lived with her wealthy brother, Yechezkiel. Chahla just moved forward, changed course, and dedicated herself to higher causes. She applied her unique

Chahla Murad and Yosef-Haim Murad, the sisters are in the background.

Chahla had many talents

leadership abilities, and spoke for the benefit of women and their rights. She proved how one could transform the community by applying the deeds of changing the world for the better (Tikun Olam). Chahla's charisma enabled her to achieve her goals, she earned the respect and trust of her family, and in turn they generously donated to benefit her causes.

Chahla had many talents; she was an accomplished dressmaker and designer of both day-to-day clothing and wedding dresses. Chahla taught young girls the art of sewing and embroidery, advised those young brides on how to solve their problems, guided the expecting women during their pregnancies and continued to mentor after their deliveries, teaching them how to raise their children and tackle health issues. Chahla continued her efforts to help individuals adjust to the community and to advance their social conditions so they could give their children proper education. As the Talmud says: "Loving kindness is greater than laws; and the charities of life are more than all ceremonies".

Chahla's Torah Scroll

In addition, Chahla, saved enough money to pay her brother, Rabbi Ezra, to write a Torah Scroll, dedicated after her. It is one of the two Scrolls that were successfully brought to Israel years later, and it was successfully restored by donations from the children of Mordechai and Khatoun Murad of our generation.

Yechezkiel (Ezkiel) Murad (1855-1938) Yechezkiel was the second son of Mordechai and Mazal. He was fondly remembered by his affectionate name Yechezkiel Ammi, which is "my uncle Yechezkiel". He was known to have performed great deeds such as "Respect your Father and your Mother", which the Ten Commandments so stresses. Yechezkiel cared for his mother Mazal and his sister Chahla, who both lived in his house.

Yecheziel Murad and Aziza Abdulanbi

Yechezkiel was also known for his hospitality (Hachnasat Orchim). His mansion was open to all, just like Abraham the Patriarch. Every Saturday, after the break of Shabbat the family would gather in his house to enjoy supper, called Seuda Shlishit. He served delicious homemade dairy dishes and pastries. These pleasant gatherings had a great impact on the family. Yechezkiel's son, Meir, continued this tradition of gathering the families with all their children every Saturday evening. The chain was not broken and the Mitzvah, or good deed of hospitality, continued.

Yechezkiel was raised by his elder brother Eliyahu, whom we lost when the tracing the records. Following the death of their father,

Yechezkiel pleaded with his brother to enroll him to study at the "Alliance School." Eliyahu feared that if Yechezkiel studied at a non-religious school, he would lose the values of Judaism, and so, was against the idea. Yechezkiel insisted on getting an education and was frequently crying and demanding that his older brother consent to sending him to the "Alliance School."

One day, a Sheikh passed by Eliyahu's office and asked him to teach his brother, in Arabic, at a private school with other students from rich and powerful families. Eliyahu agreed to this: Yechezkiel was fortunate to study at the school under the tutelage of his brother. The school was respectful of Yechezkiel's religion as seen in the following story:

> At the school, when the teacher entered the class, the students stood up and said in Arabic, "There is no God but God and Muhamad is his messenger". Yechezkiel did not stand up to recite this sentence. When the teacher asked why, Yechezkiel answered that he was Jewish, and being a Jew he cannot say it. The teacher solved this problem by changing the sentence for Yechezkiel, who could now say "There is no other God but God and Moses spoke to God."

Education empowered Yechezkiel and enabled him to achieve heights of success in his business as well as in his social life.

The Life of the Notable Rabbi Ezra Murad Hackam David (1864-1936)

Rabbi Ezra was a distinguished scholar, born to a distinguished family: The youngest son of Mordechai and Mazal, Eliyahu Mordechai's grandson, and Hakham David's great-grandson. He inherited his ancestors' wisdom and talent, making big advances in his career. Ezra held the prestigious position of a judge and a spiritual leader of the Jewish Court. His desire to become a Rabbi and to serve the community was evident from his early childhood. He studied at the Kutaab (First Seminary) and at the Istad, (the graduate seminary).

ישיבת כנסת מאיר לייהו נע

His great love for Torah and eagerness for Torah study was reflected in his personality and his glowing face. He continued his studies at Yeshiva called Meir the supervision of Rabbi Shlomo (Solomon) Laniado.

His G-d given gifts illuminated all he knew and acted as a role model for the community. He revealed his modesty, righteousness, honesty, and extraordinary humility to all. Rabbi Ezra had a phenomenal memory. He mastered and remembered all the Shulchan Aruch (the set of table), Mishna, and Aggadah. His insight was unsurpassed in the Halacha (Jewish Law) and Gemara, which encompassed many aspects of Jewish Law including right and wrong, the pure and impure, and the righteous and evil. He was like a tree of knowledge with numerous branches and thousands of leaves, all to satisfy our Torah hunger and show us the right way of life. His gift of singing captivated his audience and they went home feeling great satisfaction and enjoyment. His powerful, clear, and vibrant voice was heard beyond the walls of the Great Synagogue (Slat Le-Kbiri in Arabic).

People often visited his open house, from rich and poor to wise and simple, to receive his advice. He answered all their questions and gave advice that satisfied everyone and proved to all his deep knowledge and mastery in all areas of Jewish law. Therefore, the community accepted his decisions as final and followed his sage advice.

Rabbi Ezra's handwriting was so clear, precise, and exceptional that he wrote hundreds of Torah Scrolls, Mezuzot, Megilot Esther, and many other religious items in the classical Hebrew alphabet, all requiring the hands of an artisan. He created the wonderful Talismans and Blessings, all rooted in the Kabbala and used by many, including the sick and mentally ill, to strengthen confidence and inner joy. Even after a hundred and fifteen years, his writing on the old scrolls is still clear and readable. The speed of his writing was phenomenal; his hand sped quickly over the scrolls in a precise motion that enabled him to complete hundreds of Torah Scrolls in his lifetime. This gift of writing is rightfully compared to the level and quality of Ezra Hasofer, or Ezra the Scribe, the great writer of many centuries ago. We will introduce you his importance and contribution to Judaism in our history part.

Before writing Torah Scrolls, or any other religious items, Rabbi Ezra Murad would fast and purify his body and soul to achieve spiritual heights. He immersed himself in the Mikveh (Pure Eater Bath) situated in his home. Only then would he feel ready to start writing. Writing the Teffillin is one of the 613 Commandments-- it is a call from a higher power that must be fulfilled daily. It is therefore, a great privilege to be able to write it. Rabbi Ezra would recite the blessing, *"G-d is Blessed (Hashem Yethbarach) for allowing me to write where I can glorify His Holy Name with prayers and blessings"*. One more duty that required knowledge and ability was the writing of the Get, which is the divorce agreement, of which Rabbi Ezra was in charge for the community court (Bet-Hadin).

Rabbi Ezra conducted marriage ceremonies based on strict Jewish tradition. The demand for this service was extremely high and people appreciated the level of his performance. It became an honor to have the marriage ceremony conducted by such a reputable and qualified person. In the same manner, he also performed circumcision ceremonies, for which he also had a great demand from the people who sought professionalism.

Rabbi Ezra supervised the Slaughter (Shechita) of the animals all over Iraq, making sure that they were conducted with a preciseness that rendered the meat "Kosher." The following Hebrew blessing signified the full meaning of the Slaughter: "*Asher kideshanu be- mitzvotav vetzivanu al hashechita*". This is a blessing that praises G-d for bestowing on us the gift of eating meat. Rabbi Ezra's strong desire to perform Mitzvoth (good deeds) came from his belief that in opening your hand to satisfy another living creature, you do a great Mitzvah (great commandment). Therefore, many duties that Rabbi Ezra performed were without any financial reward, as shown in the following story:

Rabbi Ezra was a permanent visitor at Rabbi Yoseph (Joseph) Haim's household (1834-1909), who was Rabbi Ezra's mentor, advisor, and close companion. Being so close, Rabbi Ezra was able to see firsthand Rabbi Yosef's great thought and influential rabbinic writings, the most important of these was his famous work "Ben Ish Chai" (A Living Soul). He saw the importance and the contribution to Jewish thought as an asset for future generations that deserved to be published. Rabbi Ezra went ahead and printed the first edition of

"Ben Ish Chai" at his own personal expense, for no material gain to himself. The book took off after the first printing and became the standard codebook of study at Torah Academies around the world.

Rabbi Ezra revered Rabbi Yosef Haim, and after Haim's death, felt void and empty without his admired friend; he wanted desperately to keep the Rabbi's memory alive within the walls of his own family. Just eight years after Rabbi Joseph's death, Farha, Rabbi Ezra's first wife had a powerful dream in which Rabbi Yosef-Haim appeared and began speaking to her in a soft manner and said, "Farha, I am going to be your guest today" and then he sat down on a big box in her room. When Farha woke up, deeply affected by the dream, she thanked *Hashem* (G-d) for granting her the privilege of seeing the dear Rabbi, and excitedly shared the dream with her husband. The impact of this powerful vision resulted in naming their newborn boy after the great Rabbi.

Rabbi Ezra's gift of oratory, Devar Torah (Sermon) on Saturdays attracted many people who eagerly waited listening to his Drasha (Sermon). The crowd even rose in full ovation following his speech and clearly felt that it was the light of the day. These remarkable and stimulating sermons were never recycled: There was always something new and philosophical that included Aggada (legend stories) along with interpretations on various laws. Those elements were important and captured the hearts of the people who felt that their prayers were elevated and spiritually empowered. On weekdays, Rabbi Ezra spoke at Yechezkiel Synagogues in Baghdad teaching and guiding his audience along the path of Torah and Mitzvoth (great deeds).

What is Aggada? Aggada is the Biblical Hebrew blog, which is mostly recorded in the Talmud and Midrash, which is a rabbinic literature and part of Judaism's Oral Law, it includes sayings of the sages, spiritual stories, parables, and theological statements.

The Aggada also includes the legend of young Abraham smashing idols in Mesopotamia (modern day Iraq) and tells how Abraham discovered and accepted the voice of one single God. The Midrash tells us that Abraham challenged conventional wisdom, his family, his people, and the culture around him. Abraham's spiritual personality along with his revolutionary idea about G-d is a model for Jews in any age.

What does the Talmud say about personal morality such as Envy, Jealousy and Pride? ". . .that no hatred against us may enter the heart of any man, that no hatred of any man enter our heart, that no envy of any man enter our heart. Humility, is the greatest of all virtues, arrogant spirit is as though he had worshipped idols, Arrogance is not only evil trait because it hurts other people and will eventually lead to frustration."

The Rabbis concluded: "Whoever runs after greatness, greatness will elude him: whoever flees from greatness, greatness will pursue him."

What does the Talmud say about habit and Character? "A good deed, leads to another good deed, and the consequence of one transgression is another transgression." "Avoid even a minor transgression lest it lead you to a major one."

The Talmud prized the ability of some people to control their emotions. "Who is a hero?" "He who controls his passion."

What is Mishnah and Gemara? The word Mishnah means to keep on studying. Studying what? Studying the Oral Law. After the destruction of the Second Temple in 70 AD, there was a need to arrange the huge body of material known as Oral Law, to preserve Judaism and Jewish communities scattered throughout the Roman Empire. In the third century AD, Judah the Prince, the head of the Sanhedrin (Jewish Court) in the land of Israel, codified and divided the Oral Law into six orders. Each order is divided into tractates and each tractate is divided into chapters.

The Gemara interprets and comments on the Mishnah. The Gemara is a supplement on the Mishnah. In order to be able to follow Bible laws, there was a need to elaborate, supplement and clarify on its content and how to execute the laws. This creativity of those scholarly interpretations and debates formed the Babylonian Talmud.

To give you an example of how the Mishnah and the Gemara work together:

One Mishnah says: "If debris falls on someone and it is doubtful or not he is there or whether he is alive or dead, one must open the heap of debris to rescue him, even on Shabbat." The Gemara supplements: "One must remove debris to save a life on the Shabbat, and the more zealous one in doing so the more praiseworthy he is."

The Gemara continues to elaborate on saving life: "If he saw a door closing upon an infant thereby frightening or endangering the infant, he may break it so as to get the child out-the faster the better. . .One may extinguish or isolate the flames in the case of fire-the sooner the better."

RABBI EZRA BECOMES FAMOUS

All over Iraq, people accepted the authority and decisions of Rabbi Ezra as the final word of the law. He hired skilled artisans to make his specially written Talismans that were recognized by the sick and mentally challenged as having the power to heal. This stemmed from the belief that they were written by a great tzadik (a righteous man), and a man of exceptional brilliance and modesty. Thus, Hakham Ezra's name became popular, resembling a candle that lights the void.

The Rabbis of the generation had the opportunity to witness Rabbi Ezra's accomplished sermons, sharp intelligence, honesty, integrity, and modesty, as well as witnessing his huge number of followers. They came to a solid conclusion, without any doubt, about Rabbi Ezra's ability to lead the community. They unanimously decided that he was indeed a worthy Rabbi to hold the prestigious position of Chief Rabbi, and thus, Rabbi Ezra was offered this position. However, Rabbi Ezra turned down their offer. The Rabbis repeatedly asked him to accept the offer, but he repeatedly refused, not because of fear or doubt of being unable to fulfill this duty, but only out of modesty. Rabbi Ezra was most humble, and even though he was fully aware of his qualifications and accomplishments, he did not demand more for himself.

Rabbi Ezra was finally persuaded to accept the position of a judge and spiritual leader as President of the Jewish Court in Baghdad (AV Beit Hadin). This Court had legal power bestowed by the State over all personal situations, such as marriage and divorce.

THE DEATH OF A RIGHTEOUS MAN (TSADIK)

One evening, Rabbi Ezra returned home from the Synagogue and went to sleep. In the middle of the night he woke up, got out of bed, and felt dizzy and unable to control his body. He collapsed on the floor unconscious, and instantly died. Doctors could not determine the exact cause of his death. He died on Aug. 12, 1936.

The bitter news quickly spread throughout Iraq. The report shook the community and evoked a sea of tears from his large family, the Rabbis, the head of the Iraqi Jewry, scholars, and chiefs of Torah Academies. All affected had a hard time digesting his sudden passing.

His eulogy was impressive, held at the Great Synagogue (Slat Le-kbiri) in Baghdad, which was the biggest and most prestigious synagogue in Iraq. This synagogue was the only place where they could accommodate the crowds that came to honor him and pay their last respects. Five to ten thousand people attended his funeral. The Shivaa (seven days of mourning) was held at the house of Rabbi Ezra's brother, Menashe, whose residence was big enough to accommodate a thousand people a day during the seven days of the Shivaa. Rabbi Ezra was buried at the Jewish cemetery in Baghdad. The entire Jewish community mourned the loss of this great Hakham.

PERSONAL ACCOUNT OF RABBI EZRA'S LIFE

In order to better understand the life of Rabbi Ezra, the following is included as a personal account from Rabbi Ezra's son, Issac Murad, who presently lives in Tel-Aviv, Israel.

"I was only twelve and a half at the time of my father's sudden death. Therefore, this appreciation and these stories relate to a period of six or seven years of my childhood, in the years 1831-1936, especially in the last three years of his life.

Rabbi Ezra was a well-known and respected member of the Jewish community of his time. In 1933, when the Jews were asked to elect a Head of the Community, Rabbi Ezra competed with Rabbi Sassoon Kadoorie for the post.

Rabbi Ezra was one of eleven members of the Meir High Yeshiva, who received small monthly payments from the community purse.

He served voluntarily as one of the three judges (*dayan*) of the Jewish Court, which dealt with disputes between Jews according to the Torah. This Court dealt chiefly with divorces, inheritance, and minor disputes (not criminal cases), and government authorities recognized its decisions.

Rabbi Ezra also carried out some religious functions voluntarily. He gave a drasha (sermon) of two hours every Saturday afternoon and a drasha of half an hour every evening (his last one was on the night of his death). He was the Chazzan (Cantor) in a nearby synagogue, where he also read the weekly parasha (weekly section) in the Torah Scroll on Saturdays, twice: once at dawn, in the first *jafka* (group), and again second *jafka,* when he also prayed.

He also served as the Cantor of the same synagogue on the Jewish High Holidays Rosh Hashana and Yom Kippur, without payment. He conducted marriage ceremonies, and was consulted and ruled on various points of religious subjects.

In order to increase his fixed, small income, he engaged himself in various religious activities, including writing and selling Torah

Scrolls. When he died, he left one for sale with a quantity of leather for future use. He also left a mini Torah Scroll, written in minute letters, which he refused to sell. After his death, it was auctioned and bought by my brother for a sizable amount. It was left in Zilkha Synagogue, and was burnt when this Synagogue caught fire a few years later. The other Torah Scroll was also auctioned and was bought by a stranger.

Other activities for supplementing his income included the writing of Tefillin, mezuzot and Megilat Esther (the story of Esther), the sale of imported prayer books, and writing divorce documents (get), which had to be written on a special paper immediately when the divorce was declared by the Court. The get then had to be delivered to the wife in person by the husband or by proxy, as a messenger of the Court.

My father was modest and avoided disputes. When I was eight years old, he had a traffic accident caused by the bus driver, who started the bus before my father completed stepping down. When he was told to submit a complaint at the police station, he refused to do so. His hip and arm were broken and he spent six months at home, attended by a chiropractor and physiotherapist until he could function properly.

My father was extremely religious. He observed the Torah commandments and the rules of religion as far as he could. Until the last year of his life he observed all the five fasts, which Jewish law requires. After the Morning Prayer he remained in the synagogue reading the daily portions of the Torah, twice Mikra and once Targum, and specific portions of other parts of the Bible, the Mishna. At the end of his morning prayer, he always gave some change to charity.

Although he was devout, he was tolerant to the way of life of other individuals. He would not scold people for gross breaches of the rules, such as smoking on Shabbat in front of him. My brother had to work on Shabbat for his living in those years of the Great Depression and my father did not complain or try to stop him.

Friday nights my father said the Kiddush and after we had supper, the family gathered and joined in as he sang the Shabbat songs.

After the singing he told us stories of the Bible and other tales until the children were sleepy and were taken to bed.

At age three, I was sent to Istad (Nursery) where along with around ten other children we were taught to read the Hebrew Alphabet and to count. At age four, I entered the Midrash Talmud Torah, where I was taught to read Hebrew and learned Bible stories. There was a strict discipline and those who disobeyed were punished by the stick. I was not happy there, but I learnt much for my age. Since I could read, my father took me to the synagogue and taught me to pray. At age five, I entered the preparatory class at a Jewish Elementary School and continued there until graduation. During the three months of the summer vacation, my father made me go to Midrash Talmud Torah and later, to the Rabbi Shimon Yeshiva for juniors, where the pupils were taught to read Rashi and Shulchan Arukh, a set table of laws.

Since I was obedient, I also prayed every evening and in later years, also at dawn. And of course I observed the rules of religion, especially the Shabbat. On Shabbat days, we prayed in the morning and after the late morning heavy meal. I was sent to a place where portions of the Bible were read musically. After the noon prayer, which is called Minha, and a light lunch, I used to join my father at the synagogue to hear his two-hour sermon. After a short interval, the time came for the evening prayer, before which portions of the Psalms were read and Shabbat songs were sung. Coming home after the evening prayer, dinner was served and thereafter, special songs on Prophet Elijah were sung. Only then ordinary work or school tasks could be done.

Though I spent much time on religious duties, I found the time to learn the school lessons and do the school tasks and to be always among the best in the class. I only missed reading library books and some school recreations. During vacations on weekdays, I also attended my father's evening Drasha, delivered after the prayer.

When I finished Grade Four, my father thought that I had enough regular schooling and wanted me to go to the Zilkha Yeshiva. Maybe he thought I could eventually become a Rabbi. I resisted, and in order to receive his consent, I had to promise him that I would continue to pray, observe the rules of religion, and go to the Yeshiva on vacations. My father was a person of high integrity who kept to his principles. He never lost hope, always trusting God to answer his prayers. I loved and admired my father. He was my role model and his teachings molded my character and affected my behavior."

The above account serves to reinforce the inspirational and devoted life led by Rabbi Ezra.

RABBI EZRA AND FARHA'S CHILDREN

Rabbi Ezra's first wife passed away at a young age, and so Chahla raised her five children. She played a big role in their lives and they had a strong attachment to her. She treated them with love and kindness and they saw in her a mother's image and always referred to her as Ameti, meaning "my Aunt". Chahla also married them off, looked after their dowries, and helped them raise their own children.

All of Rabbi Ezra's children (a son and daughters from Farha, three daughters and two sons from Gergia) loved their father passionately. His memory would always live among them. All of Farha's children named one of their own children after their beloved father. Rabbi Ezra's children cherished the religious items that their father had written for them and deeply believed in the healing power of his writings. Let's now introduce you to Rabbi Ezra's children.

Gergia Murad-Elias (1900-1989) was Rabbi Ezra's eldest daughter. A charming and genuine girl who accepted her life without complains. Family and friends loved Gergia for her modesty and devotion to her ten children. She raised her children with the help of her aunt Chahla. Gergia never interfered with anybody's life and minded her

own business, yet she completely understood her surroundings. With her strong
willpower and determination she lost
35 kilos and maintained it! It is the pride
of our family to mention here that Gergia's eldest son Elia. Elia studied law in
Bagdad and then immigrated to England
in the late forties. Arriving to London almost penniless, just to become a Multi
millionaire a couple of years later, engag-
ing in trade import export.

Gergia Murad-Elias

Rachel Murad Aslan (1900-1975) The second daughter of Rabbi Ezra
was a teacher in Baghdad. She was unconditionally loved by her students, who helped her in the hectic preparations of her dowry. In Israel, she was unconditionally loved by her children who did everything
they could to ease the challenges she faced in her new life. On the other
hand, her devotion to her children proved to be so successful that it
paid off by witnessing their success in Israel and Montreal.

Rachel Murad and husband Sasson are celebrating their grandson's
Bar-Mitzvah

Khatoun Lulu and Mordechai Murad
with Flora, Moshe and Aaron

Khatoun Lulu Murad (1905-1985) The third daughter of Rabbi Ezra, Khatoun was known for her incredible beauty and kindness. She was educated and learned English and French. Khatoun was a wise woman, and her advice to her sisters and brother was always from the heart. She was genuine and minded her own business, and was dedicated to raising her children in Baghdad and in Israel. She married Mordechai, her first cousin, when she was seventeen. Mordechai was the son of Menashe Murad, Rabbi Ezra's brother. Mordechai and Khatoun lived in abundance; they traveled with their family throughout the Middle East, and sent their children to the best schools. They had five boys and two girls. Khatoun experienced much adversity, but tried maintain control and live a happy life.

At the age of forty-five and just one month before she immigrated to Israel, Khatoun lost her husband Mordechai. His tragic death combined with the challenges she faced in Israel affected her life. As a consequence of the turmoil before the immigration to Israel, Khatoun, our mother, lost all her husband's assets and bank accounts. She arrived in Israel a widower, with a large family to support and had almost no resources for starting over.

Rena Murad Aslan (1910-1997), The fourth daughter of Rabbi Ezra, Rena was smart and educated. She was inspirational and served as a role model for many. She acted as a backbone for her sisters and brother, and when all her nieces and nephews used to come to her for her advice, Rena was ready to help and felt responsible for every one of them.

Rena went to Israel during the mass immigration in 1951, with her younger daughter, Ruth, and her youngest son Freddie, and settled in Ramat-Gan. Rena's husband, David Aslan, remained in Baghdad for another 14 years while Rena was with her children in Israel. Rena encountered difficult situations and decisions while by herself; it was an enormous burden that she expressed once while she was crying, "I am fulfilling the role

Rena Murad Aslan, her daughter Claire Aslan Assia, graddaughter, Ourite Aslan

of a mother and a father." Despite her difficulties, Rena prevailed, and she finally was able to reunite with her husband in London where they spent the rest of their lives.

Yosef-Haim Murad (1915-1995) was the youngest son of Rabbi Ezra and Farha and was loved by all his family. His attitude was that no matter how hard his life was, he still smiled. He was the eternal optimist, even though he lost everything in Baghdad; even the hard life he experienced in the Maa'bara (transition camp) did not take away his smile of optimism. In those days, he would welcome any visiting family member as if he was welcoming them into his own castle, without any complaint about life in the Maa'bara. We all have a soft spot for Uncle Joseph. His heart was of gold; he loved everybody. His kindness and generosity were an example. He would give the shirt off his back to anyone who needed it, with a positive attitude and smile.

Worth noting the huge success of his son Ezra, excelled in technology and invented numerous patents in technology.

Left to right Josef-Haim his grandaon Tomer Morad, and the in-laws

1963 Ramat-Gan Israel, celebrating Mordechai Rehany's Pedion which has to occure one month after birth. Right: Rachel Murad, Orit Murad, Khatoun Lulu Murad, Flora Murad Haviv, Flora's children, Back from right; Saul Rehany, Aaron Murad, Emile Murad with son Mordechai, Yehudit, Moshe Murad z"l, Batia Eeny Murad.

Family faction in London at Ruth Aslan's daughter's wedding in 2007, sitting: left to right: Freddie Aslan and his wife, Ourit Assia (California, U.S.), and Gila Murad, standing: left to right: Ezra Elias son of Gergia, Ruth Aslan Ingram, Victoria Wexler (N.Y. U.S.)

RABBI EZRA'S WORK

Rabbi Ezra's Scroll

*A few of many
Mezuzoth of Rabbi
Ezra, all rooted from
Kabbala*

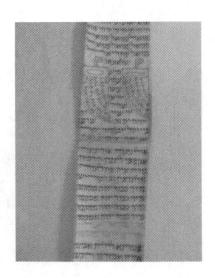

One of the many Esther Scrolls - clear writing

The Life of
Menashe Murad

*M*enashe Murad (1872-1965) was Rabbi Ezra's brother, and was sixteen years old when he married Chahla Rachel, the fourteen-year-old daughter of Haim and Hanna Tawfiq.

Menashe was living with his oldest brother, Eliyahu, at the time of his marriage. There was a dilemma confronting Menashe over where he should stay with his young wife. Options were limited, and he was forced to use the Nim (basement), the cool room on the ground floor. It so happened, that the ceiling of the Nim was too low for the bronze bed that Menashe prepared. What did Menashe do? Simple, he dug four holes in the ground to sink the bed and fit it into the low ceiling of the Nim.

Hanna Tawfiq, Rachel's mother, was a brave woman on her own merits. When she was just thirteen years old she was sent by her father, living at the time in Egypt, to go back to Baghdad to join her mother's family. She was disguised as a boy, and took an Arab Caravan from Egypt to Baghdad traveling on a camel for days in the hot sandy dessert climate. Although she must have been afraid that something terrible could happen to her, she trusted God and never lost hope to reach her destination.

In the next story we shall see how her daughter took after her, in defying conservative community customs and traditions.

Eliyahu and Toya Tawfik (dates unknown) Toya is Hanna's daughter, who married Eliyahu Tawfik. Both Toya and Eliyahu demonstrate leadership and bravery, and through them we learn about marriage traditions in Baghdad up to the immigration to Israel.

Eliyahu was a born leader, when he talked Menashe listened. People used to say, "Menashe doesn't talk only when Eliyahu is present." He was the head of the Jewish community in Baghdad. Toya, Menashe's sister in law, is 104 years old still living in Ramat-Gan Israel.

Toya is an example of how marriage used to be conducted in Iraq. Her parents decided that it was time for their naughty daughter of 15 years old to find a groom. Without consulting her, they found a well to do young man and set an engagement date. Toya demanded to see the man, even though it was unheard of in those days. However, Toya did not give up and went to the synagogue to inspect the man. She noticed that his Sisid was mended. She asked her parents afterwards, "Why would a wealthy man repair his Sisid instead of buying a new one?" This was unacceptable to her, and she refused to marry him. Her parents did not take her seriously, "she is just a little girl," they said, and continued with their preparations for the engagement. On the night of the engagement, Toya ran away to her grandmother's house. The groom's family came to the bride's house waiting for the bride, but she was nowhere to be found. The groom's family was outrageous and left the house, saying that she was a bad girl. The community discredited her for what she did, and nobody wanted to marry a girl like her.

Eliyahu Tawfik came from Singapore to Baghdad. He was forty years old, separated from his wife, and was ready to find another partner. Toya's parents thought to seize the opportunity, and brought him with the family to Israel.

Toya and Elyahu Tawfik

Toya's parents asked her if she would marry Eliyahu. She agreed to marry him and said, "I am marrying him because he is educated."

The Rabbis registered the marriage, but they were still not legally married. A few years later news came from Singapore that Eliyahu's previous wife died suddenly, so he and Toya were remarried legally. Human rights, freedom, and justice were granted only to men, and Toya was the first in our family to defying those orders. She acted as a role model for women's rights advocates.

TABLE RULES AT MENASHE'S HOUSE

Menashe was the dominant personality in the family. His children consulted him in all matters related to family and business; nothing was permitted without his approval. We called our grandfather ABI, his children called him ABUYI (my father), and the in-laws called him Ammi. The in-laws always strived to gain his favor.

At Abi's house, there were strict table manners when we sat down for lunch in the terrace on the second floor overlooking the yard. In the middle of the yard was an old Nebeg tree that reached above the roof and covered the house with a canopy of green leaves and gave many bushels of small tasty fruit every summer. Swarms of sparrows roosted on the tree every evening at dusk, and they sang their last songs of the day, filling the house with noisy chirping.

Everybody sat around the dining table waiting for their meals to arrive, while my grandmother Rachel was in the kitchen on the ground floor preparing dishes of white rice topped with stew. Then a servant took the steaming dishes to the second floor, one at a time. The first dish, which contained the biggest heap of rice, was destined for Abi. Then the dishes arrived with smaller amounts of rice, so that when it came to my turn, I received the smallest dish of all. I was seven or eight years old at the time.

Talking was not allowed during the meal except for a few occasional words. The first person that drank water from the Hub (jar) after the meal had to get a bowl of water (Tassa) for Abi, and place it in front of him. Abi did not look at the bowl placed for him, for this was a duty, not a favor. Once I was the first one to drink water from the Hub, but I forgot to get a bowl for Abi. Uncle Albert whispered in my ear and reminded me what I ought to do. Nevertheless, he did not lecture me afterwards for my forgetfulness.

Menashe showed the most leadership qualities and abilities. He knew when and where to control his emotions, he recognized that other people were his equals, and he offered honest dealings in business.

Menashe was a modernist, a westernized Iraqi Jew who mastered several languages, first and foremost of which was Hebrew. Menashe lived by the Torah. He would speak about the Patriarchs, Abraham, Isaac and Jacob, as though they were real people who lived in his lifetime. He even named two of his sons after them, Isaac and Jacob.

Yechezkiel and Menashe's Success in Business

The two brothers became partners before WWII in an import business that sold dyes for a clothing company called Johar from Switzerland and Germany. During WWII, import from Europe stopped. Yechezkiel and Menashe had a huge inventory. Prices shot up and jumped from one Gold Lira a container to a thousand Liras a container. The brothers became wealthy. After the war, they decided to split the money, and go their own ways.

Yechezkiel, known as Siedi (my master), was a Saraf (moneylender) to Jewish merchants. He used to go to work with nuts in his pocket, chewing as he walked slowly to his office. Two or three hours later, he would come back home, and two servants would run to receive him and take off his Zboon (robe) and shoes, then they would say to each other: "Siedi is tired" (my master is tired).

Meir Murad, Yechezkiel's son, took over his father's business; eventually he expanded it by acquiring American products including Wrigley's gum, Cobra shoe polish, Braso cleaning liquid and more.

Menashe's Business is Booming

Menashe became Baghdad's agent for a cigarette tubes factory located in Mosul. The cigarette tubes were sold in bundles to Arab wholesalers, who in turn sold them to street venders and small shops that filled them with tobacco and sold them to the public. Menashe had agents in the north and south of Iraq selling his tobacco products. Abi kept his stock of cigarette tubes in his office, arranged neatly along the back wall. There was a heavy desk for my father to do the accounting (blanjou) and Abi sat on a couch close to the entrance.

When an Arab customer came in, Abi would not move from his couch to serve him. After the customer said how many bundles he wanted, Abi would say, "Go get it" pointing at the back wall. On the way out the customer would pay cash, while Abi sat comfortably on the couch, and after counting the money, he would say "OK". There were no lengthy greetings, no idle talk, no thank you, and no goodbyes. All this would mean weakness to the Arabs, and showing weakness would be dangerous: They could smack him and take the merchandise without paying. Due to Abi's strict business policies, there were no incidents with the Arabs during all those years.

MENASHE'S BRAVERY DURING THE FARHOUD

At the time of the devastating Farhoud (pogrom) when the mob was attacking, killing, and looting the Jews, the mob reached Menashe's house. They knocked hard on his door and forced it open. To their surprise, as they opened the door and stood at the threshold, they were faced with an unpleasant and disturbing situation, which momentarily brought their actions to a slight halt: Menashe stood at the door waiting for them. He was defiant and fearless. He did not carry rocks, sticks or any other weapons, only his unexpected presence, his stern personality, his courageous demeanor, and his determination to stop those killers.

Menashe used the power of words only, delivered in his strong scary voice, *"Tlau men honi!"* - *"Get out of here!"* These words went far. With only a few shouts, motions of his hand for them to leave, and terse voice, he scared the mob. They turned back and ran away. But other crowds followed, larger and fiercer, and some did manage to get in and loot the expensive items in his house, such as high quality Persian carpets and other valuables. Menashe risked his own life to protect and save his family, his house and all his money which was hidden, in Sterling and in Gold coins in big jars, placed in a closed well in the basement. Parents had the authority to dictate to their children about their choices as seen in the next story. Must mention that this authority diminished upon arriving to Israel.

THE CHILDREN OF MENASHE MURAD

Habiba Murad (1896-1961) was the eldest child to Menashe and Rachel Murad. It was arranged that Meir, son of Yechezkiel Murad, should marry his cousin Habiba; however, she did not know many basic things in life, including how to comb her hair. Meir could not marry an illiterate girl since he was so well educated. Since Menashe possessed the power in the house, he insisted that his son Meir should marry Habiba, he said: "You will marry her just because I said so, and it came out of my mouth." Arranged marriages were common at the time, and there was little children could do to change the parents' minds.

Mordechai Murad (1900-1951) was highly educated, mastered five languages, and was highly intelligent. He earned his living from his partnership with his father, Menashe. They were in business together lending money to merchants and distributing raw tobacco with agents all over Iraq. Mordechai looked forward to immigrating to Israel, but G-d planned otherwise. Mordechai died an untimely, unexpectedly and tragic death at the age of 51 in Baghdad, less than one month before his family immigrated to Israel. The tumultuous environment in Baghdad and the numerous government restrictions before the mass immigration to Israel, in addition to the fear he encountered when he tried to rescue the huge amount of money in his office, caused his ulcer to open up and bleed. Within less than three days he passed. He left the legacy of an incredible human being,

Jacob Murad (1903-1999), Jacob started a business with his father Menashe, and later on he branched out on his own as a trader, securing for himself a chamber in one of the big Khans (business buildings) in the Shorga market. He supplied retailers and hotels across Iraq. He later widened his business and took a large store at the entrance of the big Khan in the Shorga (Shorga is the Jewish market). In 1935 he married Violet Meir and lived in a special wing in Menashe's large house. During the Farhoud (Pogrom) Jacob was injured while protecting his family and home. Later they moved to their own house in Bustan El-Khass, until they moved to Israel in 1951 with the mass immigration. In Israel he lived in Herzlia, which proved a wise decision when prices in the neighborhood later climbed to high levels.

Albert Murad (1912-1979) Albert was the middle son to Menashe and lived in his father's house. During his youth he contracted typhoid fever, very common in Iraq in those days. He suffered all his life from the after effects of this sickness, and he was not able to have children. Albert married his cousin Nazima, the daughter of Simcha and Nissim Cohen. After the wedding, the bride found out that Albert could not have children, and wanted a divorce. The divorce was granted fast. After the divorce, Simcha accused her sister of knowing the situation of her son, and was upset she did not disclose it before the wedding. Rachel and Menashe maintained that they did not know about their son's situation. The relations between the two families soured, and they did not talk to each other anymore. The whole community knew about Albert's situation. Menashe, the head of the family, found another girl who agreed to marry his son despite his disability. The beautiful girl was Louise Shasha. Louise was an amazing woman, always with a smile and no complaints. She loved her husband all her life; Albert had deep love and admiration toward Louise for her beauty, good nature, and understanding. They lived in Menashe's house in a special wing of their own.

Albert was a great collector and trader of stamps. This included rare stamps of countries and colonial entities that no longer exist. His collections were worth large amounts of money.

In 1951 Albert and Louise immigrated to Israel, where he bought a house together with his father Menashe, in Tel Mond. There he became a farmer. He had a grove of oranges, and a farm where he raised chickens. Later he opened a business selling school supplies in one of the rooms of their house, which was situated across the street from a school.

Isaac Murad (1919-present), attended the American University of Beirut for his high school education. Later he opened an agency business in Baghdad, representing manufacturers from around the world. Most of their products were sold in the Shorga market to wholesalers for distribution throughout Iraq. Isaac married Simha Shasha and lived in his father's house after his marriage. During the Farhoud, was injured while protecting his family and property. Isaac and his family moved to Israel in 1951 during the mass immigration of the Jews from Iraq, losing his business, bank accounts, and many of his possessions. Isaac and Simcha immigrated to Israel and lived in Tel-Aviv for the most part of their lives. Isaac enjoyed a prestigious position at Bank Leumi in Tel Aviv. The passion for working in a bank was transferred to the second generation, when Menashe, Isaac's son, established a life long career and worked at Bank Leumi until his retirement.

Ephraim Murad (1923-1996), Ephraim was named after his deceased brother who passed away, at the age of seventeen, from typhus. Ephraim the first went to Iran to avoid being drafted to the Turkish army, and while there he contracted typhus. Not many people survived the deadly disease in those days, including Ephraim. His mother mourned him, sat on the floor for the seven days of the Shivaa, wore black, and desired so badly to have another son so she could name him Ephraim. To commemorate deceased Ephraim, Menashe, asked his brother Rabbi Ezra to write a Torah Scroll in his memory. Ephraim's Scroll was not brought to Israel during the mass immigration of 1951.

The second Ephraim finished high school in Iraq at the American School for Boys, in the early forties with WWII still raging. Like most other persons of his generation, he had very limited opportunities for work or career. The situation in Iraq was slowly getting more and more difficult for Jews. The Farhoud (Pogrom) had just taken place and the Muslim-Arab Iraqi Society was getting more and more antagonistic towards the Jews. But, Ephraim was lucky. He was taken under the wing of the American principal of the school, Dr. Calvin Stoudt, who offered Ephraim a job both in the school library and as an assistant to the Principal. A year later Dr. Stoudt arranged for him to be accepted at a university in the United States to acquire higher education in engineering. He also helped him get a student visa to the US, which was difficult to get at that time, because in 1946 (just after WWII ended) US soldiers returned home and any available space in universities was first reserved for them.

At that time, it was a big hassle to get to the U.S because of the war. He had to take an unfamiliar route leaving by rail from Baghdad to the port of Basra, then by boat from Basra to Bombay, India. Then to the USA by ship, which traveled from Bombay through the Suez Canal, the length of the Mediterranean Sea, and through Gibraltar, finally crossing the Atlantic Ocean to Baltimore, Maryland. He eventually reached the college where he had been accepted, Lafayette College, and enrolled in Mechanical engineering. He graduated in 1949 with a coveted B.Sc. degree.

Aaron Murad and Ephraim grew up together. Ephraim was much like his older brother, and they used to plan their future together. But they were later separated for decades. Ephraim went to

study in the States, and Aaron was sent to complete his high school education at the American University of Beirut, The High School Section.

Ephraim became known as Frank in the US, where met and married a woman named Eleanore and had one boy and three girls. Frank joined Fairleigh Dick-inson University as a professor of mechanical engineering and held on to this job for 30 years. At the same time, he enrolled at Columbia University and received his Masters Degree in Mechanical Engineering in 1958.

Ephraim did not lack entrepreneurial spirit, even as a young boy. It was the custom to take off one's shoes before entering a home. So, there were a lot of shoes outside the door where he lived. One day he collected those shoes and went and sold one of them to a store nearby, and then bought candy with the proceeds. Later his parents had to retrieve the shoes from the retailer and pay them for the candy.

Muzli (Mazal) Murad (dates unknown), Muzli served as a role model for many. Her husband passed away at a young age, and so Muzli, as the custom was in those days, went back to live at her father's house. When in Israel, Muzli, in order to support her family, took advantage of sewing skills and started her own business of sewing at home.

Louise Murad Khashi (dates unknown) was the example of dedication. She bore a disabled child who was unable to function. She did not leave him behind in Baghdad at the time of the immigration; instead she brought him to Israel and took care of him for many years until she found a home for him.

Ramat-Gan 1961, Orit and Saul's wedding. Abi has to hoin all family weddings and pictures. Sitting: Carmella Itshaic z"l, Simcha Murad, Standing: Left: Ezra Murad, Menashe Murad, Jacob Murad, Louise Murad Kashi, Isaac Murad. Back row left: Jamil Itzhaik, Aliza Murad, Naim Murad, Emile and Batia Murad.

GOOD BYE ABI WE ARE LEAVING TO CANADA

Tel Mond 1965, Orit and Saul, Mordechai Murad Rehany as a little boy, Aaron and Tiqva, brother Ezra, Abi, Albert and Louise Murad.

Montreal 1993, get together with Uncle Jacob and family spurred many visits between the two countries, Canada and U.S. and between the two families. Lili Haviv, Guila Rehany, Uncle Jacob, Orit Murad Rehany and Vivian Murad

Uncle Jacob's visit to Montreal in 1993 Left to right: Tina Murad, Saul Rehany, Vivian Murad, Richard Murad, Jacob and violet Murad

Mordi and Rose Rehany's wedding

Some 30 years after my wedding was another wedding - my son's wedding - we are lucky to host Uncle Isaac and his wife Simcha in Montreal November 1st 1993. Sitting from left: Uncle Isaac Murad, Ola Murad z"l, Ezra Murad, dear friend Anat Obadia, dear Saul's cousin Shlomo Lamdan z"l, his wife Eileen Lamdan and wonderful Simcha Murad. Standing from left: Saul and Orit, Aaron Murad, Tina Murad, TiqvA Murad, Bride and Groom Mordi and Rose, Eli Murad, Morry Murad, dear friends Zvi and Leila Acre, Eli Obadia.

Reunion in New York

Uncle Jacob, Aaron Murad, Violet Murad, Eli Murad, Meashe and Richard Murad

THE FACTION IN ISRAEL

Isaac Murad, son Menashe, Simcha, daughters Aliza and Rachel

Now that we have introduced the essential members and legacy of our family, it is important to begin to focus on our life in Iraq. This is where our journey begins. Many generations of our family grew up and lived in Iraq. We found ourselves in a very unique position as a practicing Jews in Iraq. There was such turmoil surrounding us, but we all knew if we stayed close to the cuff and leaned upon one another for support, we would maintain a wonderful family life.

Here are just a few of the experiences each of us had while growing up in Iraq:

SCHOOLS IN BAGHDAD

AARON MURAD RECOLLECTS:

The community had its own Jewish schools in Iraq, in addition to a variety of foreign schools. My older sister, Flora, went to French school operated by an order of nuns from France. They taught everything in French, including the New Testament. My elder brother Moshe and the rest of us children were enrolled in the American School for Boys, where everything was taught in English and Arabic.

The schools were of very high esteem, and offered a higher quality of education than most other high schools in better parts of the world. However, when you graduated from High School, there were very limited options. Even if you got a university education, what would you do with it? What opportunities did you have? Unfortunately, the opportunities were slim to none.

When I was about 4 years old, I was enrolled in the "Midrash", a school where I first learned the Hebrew alphabet and the common vowels. At that time, the educational system was backwards; it promoted too much obedience and authority, and too little creativity and thought. During my preschool years, my Hebrew classroom had about 60 students. Desks of two were arranged in four rows of about 15 desks deep. The best, first in the class, would sit in the first desk in the front, to the right of the teacher. Beside him, the second, and behind them would sit the third and fourth, and so on. The last student in the class, the 60th in knowledge and performance, would be in the fourth row near the back wall. That is where I sat. I did not participate, or display my knowledge. I was shy and bored. I was half asleep sometimes. The teachers of course noticed this and they acted toward me accordingly.

One day, I was frustrated with the slow pace of the class, and I raised my hand. The teacher was surprised and allowed me to recite what was written on the board. I got up and said it all perfectly. The teacher was amazed and called me to the front. I went slowly, not knowing what next to expect: I was right. When I reached the teacher, I got the biggest slap on the face ever. The teacher was furious at me: "You know, but do not show it?," he barked. After I got my punishment, he promoted me and made me sit in the middle of the class.

At the elementary school, we would walk from home to school and back in groups of three or four Jewish students. Every day it seemed, a group of Muslim youngsters would be waiting for us around the corner, planning to beat us up with wires, which they used on us like whips. During one of those times, as I was going back home, one boy, a few years younger than me, approached while his father stood in full view, tacitly encouraging him. I was terrified. I was alone that day. *What should I do? This young youth is going to beat me up,* I thought. He approached me with confidence and impunity. When he came near me, I raised my hand, the only thing I could do, and gave him a resounding, big slap on the face. My palm covered his face completely. He was taken aback by my reaction. He expected me to accept a hit in submission. Instead, he got hit! He started crying and went back to his father, who seeing it was futile to do anything, took his son and went along.

How Music was taught in Baghdad

Aaron is one of the examples of how Music was taught in Baghdad. He says: There were mostly elementary and secondary schools in Baghdad. There was one university with a limited curriculum. It was not open to everyone, and it was hard to get accepted. They had quotas for every community and these quotas filled quickly. The standard was also questionable; mostly, you had to study abroad if you wanted to study anything. The nearest university was the American University of Beirut, in Beirut, Lebanon.

This University was a high standard university based on an American curriculum, but they did not teach every subject, and the cost was high. For example, if you wanted to study music, you would have to take private lessons. I was lucky in this respect. I had quality lessons in music when I was in elementary school. When I finished elementary school, I went to Beirut to complete my high school education.

One day, when I was in grade four of elementary school, in the American School for boys in Baghdad, a musician from Aleppo, Syria, passed by the school and offered to give private lessons in music. He was experienced in teaching students how to play a musical instrument along with some music theory. This was announced in the classes and registration began. Many students registered immediately, but I waited to get my parent's permission first. I loved the idea of playing a musical instrument. This teacher mainly taught the Oud, which is like a bulky guitar and is still very popular in the Middle East. My parents agreed and my lessons started. Eventually,

I was the only one left from all those who registered initially; they had all dropped the idea.

I studied hard at my private Oud and music theory lessons. Later, I had the idea of writing music myself. I discussed the idea with the teacher and he offered to teach me music composition for Middle Eastern music. I took the music lessons for about 18 months, 6 of which were in composition. My father believed in me and gave me the permission to go ahead. After my elementary school, I was sent to the American University of Beirut to complete my high school education. I did not take any more lessons in music after that, but I advanced on my own. I switched to violin and assembled a school orchestra. The violin exposed me to classical music, which became my favorite. Because of the great immigration from Iraq to Israel, I lost all my notes, all my scores, all my musical instruments, and never played the Oud again. In retrospect, the result of my music education was to understand and appreciate music, learn about various musical instrument's scope and limitations, and most importantly, actually compose music. This prepared me to think *I can do it.*

My brother Haim Murad and I were like twins—we played, thought, and studied together. Haim was an intellectual. He assembled a library of books at a time when they were not easy to come by because of the social climate and the war. He read many books, including all that he had assembled in his library.

Haim was named after a grandfather in the family, a tradition that all the members of the family also followed; they named their new children after the grandfather who passed away. Later, many of these children, named Haim, did not survive, and died at a young age. My brother did not like that. He decided to change his name from Haim to Salim, a word that rhymes with Haim and also means "safe." However, the bad omen caught up with him, when he contracted typhus, a common disease in Iraq at that time, and passed away at the age of 14. I did not see him in his last moments because I was studying in Lebanon, but to this very day, I have never stopped thinking about him.

THE KITE THAT REFUSED TO FLY ON TISHA B'AV

Mama (Emile recollects), the daughter of a Rabbi, was a firm believer in Judaism. She used to sing "Eshet Chail" every Friday during the day while preparing for Shabbat Dinner. After completing her cooking, she would start preparing her *koraii* (a bowl to hold the candle) for Shabbat Candles. She wrapped small palm sticks in Cotton, and placed them in the glass *koraii* (bowl) with water and sesame oil. Mama would light each of the seven sticks, raise her eyes to the sky, and solemnly say her prayers.

During the summer break, we used to fly kites that we made ourselves. This was the hobby of all the children in the neighborhood. Some of the boys would paint them the colors of various flags. These flags would include the Iraqi national flag, the British flag, the Turkish flag and even the United Stated flag with its stars and stripes. The days around Tisha B'Av were very hot, and there was no breeze, Mama used to tell me that the kite would not fly because of Tisha B'Av, and that if I did not believe it, I could try and see.

I did try. The kite would not go up in the air. It would not even budge from the ground. I went down from the roof and told Mama that she was right; the kite did not fly because of Tisha B'Av. Mama would say proudly, "You see, I told you."

BUSINESS IN IRAQ

When I (Aaron Murad) was nine years old, I was deemed ready to start learning about the world, about business, and how to make a living. One day, during my summer recess from school, my father said to me, "Aaron, come with me to my office, I want you to learn something." This would be my first insight into the inner world of business transactions.

We used to walk from our home to his office, which was situated in one of the big *khans* (warehouses) in the heart of the business district of Baghdad on a short street called "Bank Street." And true to the name, on that street there was a British Bank, called "Eastern Bank". That was the bank where most of the business people had their personal and business accounts.

They used the word "*khan*" for those very old, but sturdy, buildings that housed many businesses, both warehouses and offices. The first floor would be the warehouse, while the second had many rooms, which were rented as offices. In the warehouse, every business was assigned a corner where they put their merchandise, along with other merchants' excess stock and bulk stock. Everything was protected and accounted for by the "*Khanchi*." As the name implies, he was the manager of that "*Khan*," and he decided what to put in what corner. He knew exactly how many bundles, bags, and boxes each business had. He kept track of them mentally and was usually accurate and reliable.

At the same time, he doubled as the porter of the place. He wore a "*jindah*," a thick pad on his back, worn like a coat. Its lower part was padded thick and acted as a buffer to protect his back so the huge bags could sit securely on it and not slip down. When a jute bag was sold, he would put it on his back over the *jindah*. He would then place a wide cord made into a loop around the lower part of the sack to help him secure it, while he put the other end around his forehead. This way, his head and neck prevented the sack from slipping downward, or falling off his back. Then he would carry the sack, or a bunch of boxes, to the merchant who bought it; usually this was about 20-25 minutes walking distance.

Upstairs, they had their offices. It was usually safe, but my father, who was in partnership with his father, had a huge, and very heavy, metal safe. It was very large, the size of a full cabinet. There they put most of the money. Some of it went into the Eastern Bank, but the bulk was inside that huge safe. All dealings were in cash. My father's business was mostly lending money to other merchants. He had little merchandise. When a deal was closed, usually through the mediation of a *dellal* (sales agent), a lot of money counting occurred. The *dellal* knew both parties, and they spoke to him when they needed money. Customarily, he would make the rounds, see customers, and ask them if and when they needed money. Then he would come to my father's office to finalize the transaction. Or, conversely, when the sum of money became due, he would bring it in, usually in several bunches of cash, and then everything was counted. This was where I learned how to count cash like a cashier counts in a bank. I was good at it, very fast and accurate.

One day my father asked me to come with him to Uncle Jacob's business. I stopped counting money temporarily and went with my father. Uncle Jacob had a big store in the *shorja:* a covered long street in the midst of Baghdad, which was some old version of today's shopping mall, but displayed only variety merchandise and food. Clothes were sold only in its northern part, on the other side of the main road, Rasheed Street. In the *shorja* you found mostly wholesale businesses. It had many *khans* with shops and offices, as described earlier. Uncle Jacob had his business, a big store situated at the entrance of the huge *khan*. He sold a variety of merchandise, and many retailers and wholesalers came from out of town to replenish their stock.

He took me on to work as an apprentice, and of course, I was not paid. I worked there for the rest of the summer recess, and apprenticed again during the next one. I would mind the store while my Uncle went out on errands. I helped open boxes, stock the shelves, and kept an eye out to make sure nothing was missing or stolen. It was a good experience to be in that store. I saw people from different backgrounds, different beliefs, and different approaches to life.

FLORA

I (Orit Murad) was eight years old when my sister got married. I remember when my parents wanted to marry Flora off, the matchmakers would come to the house and speak with my mother, giving her a description of the man they were representing to offer to Flora. The procedure was the description of the groom, then Maina (introducing) would follow, and if the first visit was ok, both families agreed on the amount of money or dowry, and all the wedding details would be worked out before the groom's family sees the bride's family at her house. If this visit was successful, and the groom was happy with the bride's look and the way she carried herself, then the parents would start talking about another visit or another introduction for the couple. If this were satisfactory, then the families would proceed with the plans of the engagement and the wedding.

Before Flora's wedding, the dowry was negotiated, which included furniture, bedding, henna, and the type of wedding. Flora's clothes were elaborate. Her new dresses caught everyone's eyes, especially the beautiful floral Lilac dress with ornate designs. Some of the dresses were hand sewn and some were bought, but all of them were unique. Her bedding was embroidered with silk and cotton fabrics, and had handmade embellishments that turned the house into a small garden.

Flora's dowry was so rich

THE CELEBRATION OF THE HENNA

The highlight of weddings was the Henna night. Entertainment which included belly dancers, music and decadent meat. The tradition of the Henna has been practiced for thousands of years. The reddish dye comes from the plant called Lawsonia Alba that grows in several places in Israel and the Middle East. In the Bible, henna is referred to as "campfire." It is mentioned in the Talmud as a remedy for diseases of the urinary organs. In the Song of Solomon 4:13, it says,

"Thy plants are an orchard of pomegranates, with pleasant fruits: camphir, with spikenard"

The Mishna mentions henna as the rose among the aromatic plants that grow in Israel. Throughout the ages, people of the east

Montreal 1985—Henna celebration at the Ben-Mergue house in Cote-St. Luc left to right: sitting Alex and Yehuda Ben-Mergui Guila Rose & Mordi Rehany, standing left to right Charles Matarasso, Claire Ben-Mergui, Loly Ben-Nergui, Sam Ben-Mergui, and Mireia

Henna celebration for Mordi Rehany and Rosie Ben-Mergui is being celebrated in Montreal according to the Morrocan tradition

prized this beautiful, fast dye, which they used for dying the hair, palms of the hands, nails, and even the teeth. The Jews of Iraq, Yemen, Morocco, and other Middle Eastern Jewish communities also celebrate the Henna Night.

THE UNSATISFIED HUSBAND

I often heard women inquiring about "Just Married" couples, wondering if the bride was already expecting. The expectation was for the bride to get pregnant *Men Lelt A-dachla*, which means conceiving on the first night of the wedding. To everyone's happiness, Flora got pregnant on the first night. That meant that another soul would soon join us and come into our world. To my father, who was happy for the arrival of the baby, it meant another dowry for the newborn. Furniture, baby supplies, baby wardrobe, and if it is a boy, the cost of the birth and the brith (circumcision) would be on him. Flora was huge during her pregnancy and had a hard time during labor.

Flora was huge during her first pregnancy. Standing from right our father Mordechai and Khatoun Murad, Flora Murad and Meir Haviv. Sitting Orit and Ezra Murad

At the hospital, my uncles, father and grandfather were praying for Flora's easy and safe delivery. There was nothing else to do except pray; Flora was in a serious condition. The good news came the next day; Flora finally gave birth to a baby girl. Not a BOY!! Why was Flora's husband Meir Haviv not happy? Because he would have preferred a boy. Boys were preferred over girls, especially as the first-born. Girls were considered a burden on the family. From the time of the girl's birth, the family started to save money for her dowry. Therefore, boys were preferred. Every woman's satisfaction would be giving birth to a boy, and other women would wish her to make her seven boys, *Inshalla et-suwehem sabaa, My mother had five boys. . .*

May you make them seven boys

The Murad family is strong and successful, with many brightly colored threads woven together in a blanket of love and understanding. I hope you have enjoyed our stories and lessons, and I thank you for supporting our legacy.

Part II
The History

"My heritage has been my grounding,
and it has brought me peace."

—Maureen O' Hara

The Murad family has had an extensive and fruitful journey. The heritage is strong, and the history runs deep into the roots of its tree. Much of the current day history starts when we were children in Iraq. In order to understand the Murad family and how life developed in Iraq, it is important to understand the history of the region.

The Middle East is an eclectic and diverse community consisting of people from all walks of life and all upbringings. Within this group, there was a small but close-knit group of Jewish people who called the Middle East home. At least that was what we thought. Through our family, our home was filled with love and support. However, outside of our home, we were often times met with anti-Semitism and constant struggles. Eventually we left the Middle East to replant our seeds in Israel. However, this is the story and more important, the history of our time in the Middle East.

Early History of the Middle East

In the early days of the Middle East, people were very affected by invaders looking to conquer nations and acquire more territory. Mesopotamia, or "the land between the two rivers" was historically dubbed "The Cradle of Civilization." This land was critical to the beginnings of the Sumerians; a civilization that created a glorious history that would later benefit all of humanity.

According to Biblical parables, the Sumerians enjoyed a certain relationship with the Jews and Judaism, specifically during the great 40-day flood known in the Bible. According to archaeologists, serious floods occurred in Mesopotamia between 4000 and 2000 BC. and even appeared in the Epics of Gilgamesh, one of the first literary masterpieces. In this story, to appease the wrath of god, a great flood came and destroyed the city. The god of Ea advised Utnapishtim to build a ship for his family and animals and stay there throughout the seven days of the flood until the ship came to rest on a mountaintop.

Likewise, the flood in the Bible had its origins among the peoples of Ancient Mesopotamia. It was reshaped into a narrative about God and his purposes for mankind. The Bible calls Mesopotamia "Aram Naharaim" meaning the land between the two rivers. Mesopotamia gave birth to the concept of "empires," by conquering land and spreading culture Powerful ancient empires of Sumerians, Acadians, Assyrians and Babylonians led the foundation of the early history of the Middle East.

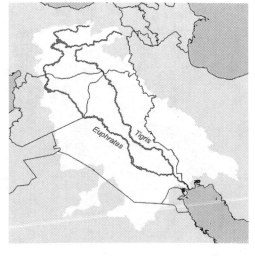

Map of Mesopotamia

In 2340 B.C. the Acadians under Sargon leadership conquered Sumer's city-states south of Mesopotamia and united its territory under one ruler and became the World's first empire. In 1800 B.C. the Amorites conquered Mesopotamia and built their own cities.

The Assyrian Empire came to power in Northern Mesopotamia seeking new lands, and conquered all of Mesopotamia. The Assyrians invaded the small kingdom of Israel, dispersed the ten tribes of Israel throughout their empire, and tried to assimilate them into the Assyrian culture. The story of the Ten Lost Tribes of Israel is recorded in the Bible.

In 1792 B.C., the Babylonians arose and conquered Assyrian cities creating the Babylonian Empire. As the Bible records, the Babylonians, under Nebuchadnezzar's rule, invaded the kingdom of Judea in the 6th century BC (586), destroyed Jerusalem and its Holy Temple, and exiled the people to Babel.

In modern day Iraq there are still ethnic groups that can trace their origins back to ancient times, such as Assyrians or Armenians. The Aramaic language, which is spoken by Armenian communities today, was the most popular language in ancient times, up to the arrival of the Muslims in the Middle East.

The Impact of the Prophets on the Babylonian's Jewish community

ollowing the destruction of the First Temple, prophet Ezekiel who was among the exiles, began to preach to the community. The community longed for their homeland of Zion, wished to be free people in their own land, mourned the loss of their Temple. They blamed this catastrophe on their own sin of turning to idolatry. The impact of the prophets on the community at the beginning of their road in Babel, was enormous. They found the relief and guidance, that they desperately needed, in their two great prophets: Jeremiah and Hezkiel, to whom they paid their utmost respect.

PROPHET YECHEZKIEL (586 BCE)

Both Prophet Ezkiel and Prophet Jeremiah foresaw the destruction of the Temple. Jeremiah bitterly criticized his people for forsaking God and the Torah by turning to idolatry. He was in

Tomb of Prophet Ezkiel

favor of surrendering to the mighty Babylonians, but the people did not take his advice, they viewed it as weakness. In the diaspora, Jeremiah preached to the exiles, "Build your houses and dwell in them, plant your gardens and eat their fruit, and seek peace, and pray to the Lord for peace".

Ezkiel preached the powerful idea of hope, and instructed his disciples never to give up the hope of returning to Zion and rebuilding the Temple.

THE PERSIAN EMPIRE AND HUMAN RIGHTS

The Persians defeated the Babylonians in 539 BCE, and under the rule of Cyrus the great (600-529) the Persian dynasty of the Achaemendis was created. Why is the arrival of the Persian Empire, is so important to remember? The arrival of the Persian Empire was crucial to the Jews. Cyrus the great not only believed in humanitarian and democratic approaches to minorities, he respected their customs and religions. For the Jews living in Babel, Cyrus issued a powerful decree for the right to return to the homeland and the right to re-build the Temple in Jerusalem. Cyrus rightfully earned honor from the Jews.

About 70 years later, a large number of Jews from Babel and Persia answered the call of Ezra the Scribe to go to the homeland. Ezra became the spiritual leader, and Nechemiah became the governor of the renewed community in Zion. The hope of return to the homeland prophesied by Ezkiel, materialized.

EZRA THE SCRIBE (480-440 BCE)

Ezra the Scribe played an important role in reshaping Judaism. In the early days of the exile, Judaism went through a transformation and became a system of ideas and a way of life. Ezra the Scribe instituted many reforms, mostly for the revival of Judaism and the study of the Scriptures. Ezra the Scribe rewrote the Sacred Records, restored Jewish Law, and codified the first four books of the Bible and the book of Deuteronomy, which together make up the five books of the Torah.

Tomb of Ezra the Scribe

The Torah became now available to the masses

Ezra's great achievement is to bring the Torah to the masses.

Ezra emphasized the importance of reading from the Torah as well as the interpretation of the Scriptures. He established the custom of reading from the Torah on Mondays, Thursdays and Saturdays, with no less than three days in between each reading.

THE BUILDING OF THE FIRST SYNAGOGUE IN BABEL

The building of the Great synagogue and the development of the concept of paryers replaced the Sacrifices in the Temple. The Great Synagogue or Slat le-kbiri in Arabic was built and it served an important and crucial element for communal life and worship. From that time on, the love for teaching and learning the Torah was developed in great proportions.

The study of the Holy Scriptures played the most important role in the community's lifestyle and worship, therefore religious study centers emerged that led to the establishment of Torah Academies. Those Academies located in Sura and Pombedita in Babel, had high

levels of influence that dealt with methods of commentary on the
Bible As a consequence, the basis of the Babylonian Talmud was
formed, which led to the compilation of the Talmud.

The compilation of the Babylonian Talmud stretched for several
centuries, from the early third century to about the sixth century BC.
During the sixth and seventh centuries, the Babylonian Talmud was
enlarged. Which created interest and responsible for the spread of
Greek Science in the rest of Europe.

There are two pictures of this synagogue, and these are the only
pictures in existence. These pictures were taken by David Sasson
around the year 1915, and were published in his book Masa'a Babel.
When the Babylonian Museum in Or Yehuda, Israel, built a model of
this synagogue, they copied the details from these two pictures. The
museum used the book Masa'a Babel for other research and stories. The
great synagogue was known to draw over 2,000 people for services.
Women sat upstairs while men prayed in an open courtyard. A Tevah
(platform) stood in the center of the courtyard with surrounding bekh-
alot (bays) for the congregants and for the Torah Scrolls. Prayers began

before dawn, and the head of household or an appointed community knocker would wake up the families before dawn for the services. He would walk the streets of the Jewish Community while screaming at the top of his voice, to awaken the sleepers for the prayer.

The beginning of Torah study and the establishment of Torah academies is known as the first Torah Golden Age. The population of the Babylonian Jewish community, during the time of the first Torah Golden Age, was greater than the surrounding population. During the Torah Golden Age the influence of the great Torah academies of Sura and Pombedita (modern-day Fallujah) was powerful. This first Golden Age lasted more than a thousand years. Its influence reached all Jews in the Diaspora as far as India, East Asia, North Africa, and Europe. The Torah academies dealt not only with the compilation of the Babylonian Talmud, but also dealt on its interpretations and the initiation of the study of science. This study of science was derived from the basis of the Hebrew calendar, which coordinated the cycle of the moon and the sun to determine the Jewish holidays. As a consequence, the study of Greek science was renewed and heightened among the Jews, which created interest of studying in the rest of Europe.

THE MUSLIM EMPIRE

The Muslims arrived to the Middle East in the early 7th century, they were very dynamic society and brought transformation to the Middle East. The Muslims brought transformation to their Empire, and the first ethnic group that benefited and excelled in the Muslim world, were the Jews.

Let's not forget that the Jews, due to their knowledge of the Torah, Talmud and Mishna, and their ability to read, had the advantage to progress in the Muslim world and were the first to collaborate with the Muslims than the rest of the population. Demand for skilled people was high, supply was low, therefore, the Jews were the first to be able to transform themselves from agrarian agricultural occupation to skilled urbanized occupations. The Jewish community stayed close-knit and vibrant, culture flourished and was integrated with the Muslims'. The estimated number of the Jewish population living in the region of Babel was one million, so the measure of its influence was high. Under the Abassid, the Jews continued to prosper and gradually they gave up the Aramaic language and adopted Arabic.

The first half of the fourteen century reflected the beginning of the decline of the Jewish community, a period that lasted about four centuries.

THE EFFECT OF THE MONGOL EMPIRE AND THE GREAT FLOOD

The 13th century brought major changes to Asia as well as the Middle East in two catastrophic events that left its mark on the Middle East for a long time to come. As such, the Murad Family was unable to trace their records prior to the 17th century. The reason can be explained in two great, catastrophic events that affected the Middle East for a long time to come.

The First Event was the arrival of the Mongols from Eastern Asia, to the Middle East in the 13th century when Genghis Khan led his army to conquer the region. The Mongolian army was the strongest army of its time, and well-trained soldiers mercilessly ruined other nations on their way to the Muslim Empire. The Mongols aimed at putting an end to the flourishing and brilliant Muslim Empire, to unseat the Muslim Abbasid Caliph in Baghdad, and to destroy Baghdad and its brilliant cultural center, schools, colleges, and libraries. The Mongols also ruined Baghdad's advanced agricultural developments including a networking canal that had existed for thousands of years, since the time of the Sumerians, when they built irrigation canals to serve the region. This catastrophic event ended the Muslim Empire's growth, not only physically but also psychologically, and the area never returned to the former glory of the Muslims in Baghdad. Consequently, Islam went through its own transformation and shifted toward conservatism, creating the beginning of the first conflict and rift between Sunni and Shia.

THE GREAT FLOOD

The second catastrophic event occurred in the 17th century which in turn caused epidemics, both of which altered the course of Babel's history.

To understand how the two rivers function we must explain where they start and how they end.

Iraq lays East of Syria between the Zagros and Kurdish mountains and the Arabian Desert. The plain in the area is fertile, and it derives its fertility from two rivers, the Tigris and the Euphrates. The valley, which spreads alongside these rivers, is referred to in the Torah as Shinar, or Naharaim. The Euphrates is the larger of the two rivers, and originates in the mountains in Northeastern Turkey. The Tigris flows from North to South and originates in the mountains of Kurdistan.

At their source, the two waterways are far from one another but they draw closer as they reach south Iraqi soil, and as the rivers stream they pick up fine earth, topsoil, and plants. When the land is high and flow is rapid, the current beneath the waves flows along seaward, and when the rivers reach lowlands, the topsoil settles in the riverbed. In the spring, when the mountain snow melts, the level of the riverbeds raises so much they become almost equal with the valley. The amount of water in the rivers increases and floods large areas of land, enriching the valley with fine earth and topsoil. When the floodwaters subside, the land becomes easy to cultivate for planting.

Unfortunately, between the years of 1826-1833, nature changed its course and the rivers vigorously flooded the valley lands, sweeping entire cities, washing away houses and property, and impoverishing thousands of families. Stagnated muddy swamps brought unfamiliar diseases. The plague came to be known by an Arabic name, Waba, or Abuzua, which is roughly translated as vomiting and watery diarrhea that led to rapid dehydration and death.

The big plague in Babel reached its highest point in 1829, when the number of dead reached 1200 people per day from the local community alone. The plague extended from northwest to southeast, and the total number of deaths is estimated around 20,000; it continued sporadically after 1833 in other parts of Mesopotamia, but with less severity.

During those long seven years, the Jewish community was affected and many Rabbis died. People abandoned their homes in Baghdad and fled to the desert. When the exodus began, many begged their Rabbis to join them, but the Rabbis and the courts did not budge. "Let our lives serve to atone for all of Iraqi Jewry," one Rabbi declared. When the people later returned to their homes, they learned their Rabbis and court members were among the victims. The people used the plague as an almanac, and when referring to family events such as births or deaths they would say, "so many years before the Waba, or so many years after the Waba."

A FUNCTIONING COMMUNITY

The community was eloquently organized since its beginning. The Bible records, that the cream and the elite of the Judean society went to Babel and that it included King Yehoiachin and other prominent Priests that were serving in the Temple in Jerusalem. King Yehoiachin became the firstexilarch or leader of the community. All other Exilarchs following him throughout the ages were chosen from King David lineage. They headed the community in Babel and held an enourmous power.

At the time of the great academies of Sura and Pompedita, the exilarch continued to lead the community and a spiritual leader which was chosen from the great Torah Academies. The exilarch were always descendant of King David, who had great power to intercede with the country's ruling government; Jewish communities all over the diaspora accepted the exilarch decisions.

The arrangement of the exilarch and a spiritual leader remained in effect throughout the Golden Age of the community, and over the next one thousand and 500 years up to the Mongol arrival.

In the 15th century the Mongol Empire made the first changes in lowering the status of the two rulers. The Mongol Tamerlane deposed the exilarch from power and replaced them with a president who was assisted by a Rabbi.

In the 16th century the Turkish Empire implemented more changes to the leadership status and in the 19th century (1849) The institution of the president and a Rabbi was abolished, with both positions united into one; the office became known as Hackam Bashi, or Chief Rabbi. The Hackam Bashi resided in Constantinople, and interceded with the Turkish government. The Chief Rabbi held the power to punish anyone transgressing the Laws of religion or even rebelling against the Turkish government.

SPANISH JEWISH CENTER IS TAKING OVER

During the period of the Mongols, the spiritual status of the conununity in Babel deteriorated Although thecommunity's submission to certain laws and taxes spared the Jewish institutions, their spiritual life could not regain its former status amid the ruins of Baghdad. As a result, many Rabbis moved to the new Jewish center of Spain, which was ruled by the Umayyad Muslim dynasty. Under the rule of Abd al-Rahman I in 755 AD, the Spanish Jewish center continued to grow culturally and intellectually enriched. Spain attracted people from all over the Muslim Empire, as there was a mosaic of people taking advantage of the opportunities in the region. The positive energy prevailed and promoted creativity and inspiration. The Jewish center of Spain became the most illuminated and important Jewish center, marking the beginning of the Golden Age. Collaboration between Muslims and Jews took place, and many cooperated and worked together as a team in various fields. The area of language and grammar skills paved the way to Arabic and Hebrew literature, Biblical studies increased, and Greek science and philosophies were stimulated. For about 200 years Jews occupied professions in medicine, commerce, finance, and agriculture.

Under Christian Spain, (974-1300 AD) the community lived relatively free, until the turning point between the years 1300-1391 that brought persecutions and forced conversions and expulsion. Many of the Jews from Spain scattered seeking refuge, and found it in the up and coming Ottoman Empire.

LIFE OF THE OTTOMAN JEWS

The Jews, who had just been expelled from Spain, in the year 1492, were welcomed to the Ottoman Empire. In return Spanish Jewry supported the Ottomans and assisted them in capturing more cities and territories. Spanish Jews were knowledgeable in the production of arms, and were considered to be very valuable to the Ottoman army. They concentrated in four major Turkish cities: Istanbul, Izmir, Salonika and Tsfat (Israel). Their prosperity and creativity rivaled that of the Golden Age of Spain under Muslim rule. Jewish literature flourished, and Joseph Caro (1488-1575), one of the most significant leaders in Rabbinic Judaism, compiled the book called "Shulkhan Aruch." The work is a code of Jewish law and is the most authoritative legal code of Judaism. Shlomo Ha-Levi Alkabes, one of the greatest Kabbalists, was born in Salonika around 1500 and made the journey to Safed; he composed the song "Lekha Dodi", a welcoming hymn for the Shabbat. Rabbi Abraham Ben Isaac Assa, born in 1710 in Istanbul, is one of the leading figures in the Golden Age and became known as the father of Judeo-Spanish literature. Most of court physicians were Jewish, Jews largely carried out Ottoman diplomacy, and held many high-ranking political positions. Well known Jewish women, such as, Dona Gracia Mendes Nassi, and Esther Kyra had a great influence on the courts.

Babel, under the Turks, was once again populated and reconstructed. The Jewish community returned to a period of prosperity and spirituality. A Second Golden Age began during the 18th and 19th centuries. A Torah study renaissance flourished and many Torah Academies were established.

The most prominent personality at the beginning of the 19th century was Rabbi Abdullah Somekh, who founded Torah Academies all over Babel that reached as far as India and the Far East. Spirituality was restored and reached the level that existed before the Mongol destruction. Rabbi Yosef (Joseph) Haim was the most accomplished student that Rabbi Abdulla Somekh produced. Rabbi Joseph-Haim later became the Chief Rabbi of Baghdad, and wrote many books that became standards of study in Torah Academies. Rabbi Joseph stunned the community and the world alike; he stressed the importance of Shabbat and introduced a ban against any violators.

WRITING TORAH SCROLLS IN BAGHDAD

Ever since the early days of the community in Iraq, there were many scribes who wrote Torahs. The scrolls were put in decorated cases ornamented with gold and silver. Many Scrolls were sent to other Jewish centers, such as Mosul in the north of Iraq, Damascus in today's Syria, and even to Tsfat in today's Israel. A large number of Scrolls were sent to Tsfat after the earthquake of 1837. In the middle of the 19th century, during the Ottoman rule, there was a period of deep economic depression. Scribes stopped writing due to the lack of funds. Later, as the economic situation of the community improved, the scribes started writing again and the synagogues started getting new Torah Scrolls.

The Great Synagogue, in Arabic called Slat L'kbiri, was still using one Torah Scroll donated by the renowned philanthropist David Sasson, on his visit to the community many years earlier. His Scroll was still being used on Rosh Hashana and Yom Kippur, the Jewish High Holidays, based on an agreement held with the donor.

Other local donors donated new Torah Scrolls, and wanted theirs to have a chance to be used on the High Holidays, but the Rabbis in the Great Synagogue said that the agreement with Sasson should remain in effect.

The arguments continued without a final decision until they referred the matter to the Rabbis in Istanbul who ruled that the agreement must continue, and should remain in effect. David Sasson's grandson, also named David Sasson, was born in India, and traveled to Iraq in 1915 to see firsthand the cradle of his family's traditions. When he visited the Great Synagogue in Baghdad, he was surprised to see that the Rabbis were still arguing about his grandfather's Torah Scroll. Moved and impressed, he went back to India and decided to write a book called "Massa'a Babel" in Hebrew, or "The Journey to Babel" in English. In this book he described the Great Synagogue and his visit to Baghdad. The book proved to be an important historical document for the Babylonian Jewry's Museum in Israel. They relied on many of its facts when they started building the Museum.

This story shows that the Jews of Iraq traditionally put great importance on their Torah Scrolls. The great majority of this community were believers. Donating a Torah Scroll in the memory of a loved one was routine. Later, the synagogues had so many it was impossible to use them all. The number of Torah Scrolls in Iraq may be in the thousands. When the immigration to Israel started in 1950, those families who had Torahs in the synagogues decided to bring them along. Thus, hundreds of precious Torahs written by dedicated and famous Iraqi Scribes arrived in Israel.

TURKEY'S DECLINE

Turkey's empire lasted 400 years. The richest periods of the empire occurred in the first 200 years, followed by the period of decline and dismantle. In the 19th century, Turkey was involved in wars with several European Powers: Britain, France, Austria-Hungary,

Italy and Russia. Turkey was losing its European territory with only the Middle East and North Africa still under Turkish rule.

Her problems stemmed not only externally but also internally, as seen in the following examples:

1. Diverse and dispersed population caused by a growing nationalist movement in several areas of the Empire.

2. Ethnic groups such as Assyrians, Armenians, Kurdish, Greek and Circassians demanding separation.

3. Turkey's alignment with Germany in the beginning of the 20th century.

4. Unfair treatment of Jews during the end of the 19th century.

The shifts of policy were viewed as dangerous to the interests of Britain and France, especially those that included the Middle East, India and Egypt, which contained a vital passage, the Suez Canal.

The Allied nations were deeply angered by Turkey's alliances, and decided to enter the war against Germany and Turkey to dismantle the Turkish Empire, to conquer the Middle East, and to create Arab and Jewish nations living side by side. The British struck an agreement with the Jews called the **Balfour Declaration** in which the British government declared its support for the establishment of a Jewish national home in Palestine.

THE BRITISH MANDATE IN THE MIDDLE EAST

In 1917, just five weeks after the Balfour Declaration, British troops led by General Sir Edmund Allenby took Jerusalem and all of Palestine, succumbing all Arab lands to British and French control. The Turkish Empire's fate was imminent and its disintegration determined by the Allied Powers, was to end its 400 years of rule and divide the area into sovereign states. In this transformation of the Middle East, the British created fourteen sovereign Arab states and one Jewish state.

A BRIEF HISTORY OF IRAQ

Iraq was carved out of the Ottoman Empire, and with its new name came a Hashemite Monarch that was chosen by the British. When defining its borders, the British did not take into consideration the politics of the different ethnic and religious groups in the country, particularly those of the

World War I

Kurds, Shiites, and Assyrians who were fighting for independence. Britain did not reform the Ottoman army either; they continued with the same operation. Sunni officers, who served under the Ottomans and dominated he higher ranks in the Turkish military, continued to serve and dominate in the Iraqi military under the British Mandate, while the Shia dominated the lower ranks. Therefore, nationalism and division among the Muslims in Iraq was rising and creating an immense pressure on the Monarchy.

In 1920, Iraq became a member of the League of Nations under British control. In 1922, the British transformed Iraq into a modern nation before granting it independence. In 1927 came the discovery of the huge oil fields near Kirkuk, north of Iraq, that brought economical improvement, making Kirkuk the center of Iraq's oil industry. In 1932, Iraq won independence from Britain and was admitted to the League of Nations. Feisal the First was proclaimed the king of Iraq, and allowed the Jewish community to send a Jewish delegation to represent their people. Other Jews played a key role in establishing the Iraqi Judicial and postal systems, the railways, the customs bureau, and many were dominant in the chamber of commerce. King Faisal was friendly to the Jews and treated them with respect. He visited Jewish institutions, Jewish schools, and met with Jewish leaders.

King Faisal the First signed the famous Faisal/Weizsman agreement to establish a national home for the Jews in Palestine. The implications of this agreement showed that two leaders and two different nations could reach an understanding in regards to their demands. Even though the Monarchy in Iraq created a period of stability, it failed to win public support and the confidence of the younger generation. The new generation of leaders was opposed to the older generation's leadership policies. There were specific disagreements with unpopular foreign policy, such as the alliance with Britain, and participation in the Baghdad Pact to establish a United Arab Republic.

RISE OF ANTI-SEMITISM IN IRAQ

The peaceful and tranquil environment during the reign of King Faisal I ended when he died from a sudden heart attack. He was succeeded by his 21- year-old son, Ghazi, whose inexperience led to a tumultuous reign marked by constant tensions between civilians, their leaders, and the army. The nationalist movement viewed the monarchy as a British puppet. General Nuri Al-Said became Prime Minister.

The Sunni-Shia conflict escalated and caused further division in the country. The Shia feared Sunni domination in the government and the army. This sectarian conflict shook the monarchy. We must remember that Europe, during the years of 1933-1945, was under Hitler's rule and Nazism. So Ghazi was Pro-Nazi and Anti-British, and became an ally of Germany. The rise of Nazism and fascism appealed to the Arabs as a way to overthrow the British. With the support of Germany, the political climate began to change. Nazi propaganda and hatred of the Jews was accelerating. Jews were accused of supporting Zionism and taking part in a Zionist plot to dominate the Middle East.

And we must remember that Zionism was a movement that started in Europe, and believed the only way to find a solution and an answer for the Jews was to establish a home in the land of their ancestors, Israel. A new chapter in the political arena was yet to unfold.

Ghazi's rule lasted until 1939 when he died in a sudden car accident. Some suspect that this could have been the work of the British; he was 27 years old when he died. His four-year-old son, Faisal II, was too young to rule, thus Faisal II's uncle Abdul el-Ilah assumed power as regent and Crown Prince of Iraq. Under the direction of the new Prime Minister Rashid Ali el-Gaylani, a Nazi sympathizer, the formation of a new cabinet brought further anti-Semitism and pro-Nazism. During WWII, Prime Minister Rashid briefly deposed Abdul el-Ilah (who was pro-British) and collaborated with another Nazi sympathizer, the Mufti of Jerusalem, Haj Amin el-Husseini. Haj Amin was a Palestinian cleric appointed by the British as grand mufti of Jerusalem, and also allied himself with Nazi Germany and thus inspired a group of politicians and army leaders to seize power from the Iraqi army.

Haj Amin was born in Jerusalem in 1925 and died in Beirut, Lebanon in 1974. He was a Sunni nationalist and a Muslim leader in the British Mandate of Palestine. He opposed Zionism and the right of the Jews to live in their homeland. He led riots and revolts against the Jews, Zionism, and the British. During WWII, he was involved in recruiting support in the Arab world for Nazi Germany. He considered Jews in the United States, UK, and the Soviet Union as aggressors against the entire Muslim world. In 1937 he was wanted by the British, but successfully fled to Lebanon, Iraq, Fascist Italy, and then to Nazi Germany where he met Adolf Hitler in 1941. Al-

Husseini requested Hitler to back Arab independence and oppose the establishment of a Jewish national home in Palestine. To execute his goal in Iraq and the Arab world, Haj Amin used youth organizations. The German Embassy in Baghdad was supplying money, books, and films to benefit his cause. *Mein Kamph* was translated to Arabic, and successfully appealed to the masses, fueling a Nazi environment.

Germany was in need of obtaining oil from Iraq for use on the Russian front, and collaborated with the Mufti of Jerusalem. The Pro-Nazi government of Rashid Ali Al-Gaylani, staged a military coup against Abdul el-Ilah's pro-British government and formed a new nationalist government, allowing the Mufti and the Arab press to rally against the Jews and accuse them of taking part in a Zionist plot to dominate the Middle East. The Nazis, on the other hand, trained soldiers in genocidal tactics.

THE POGROM

The atmosphere of hatred toward the Jews reached its peak in the pogrom during the two days of the holiday of Shavuot in 1941. Thousands of Jews became suddenly defenseless. Over 200 people died (some say even a lot more), 2000 Jews were wounded (many seriously), and at least 6500 Jews became homeless. Many women were raped. The police did not engage in protecting the Jews or stopping the savagery. These numbers, comparatively low to that of the Jews who suffered in Europe during the same period, cannot convey the reality of this horrific event. The psychological and political impact was intense. The Farhoud served as a wakeup call for the Jews, it shook the community at its core. It meant facing a bitter reality about their existence in Iraq, and it was the beginning of the end of their presence in the land that they had called home for 2600 years.

ANOTHER WICKED MAN

The Mufti encouraged Hitler to exterminate the Jews and advised him on how to carry out the travesty. The Mufti was very clear in his statements of hatred, *"Kill the Jews wherever you find them. That pleases Allah"*. . .*"The Holocaust was owing to the Jews."*. . .*"Their selfishness is rooted in their belief that they are the chosen people of G-d"*. During an interview with the German newspaper *National-Zeitung*, the Mufti declared, *"The entire Arab world now wished an Axis victory in the war, as they had common enemies in the Jews, the English, and the Bolsheviks"*

In the summer of 1944, the Mufti approached Germany, Romania, Bulgaria, and Hungary requesting to expedite the extermination of the Jews by sending them to Poland's Nazi death chambers.

In 1948, after Jordan occupied East Jerusalem, King Abdulla officially removed Al-Husseini from his post as Mufti and banned him from entering Jerusalem.

TURMOIL CONTINUES

More turmoil and instability were underway. The mass Exudes of about `150.000 Jews was completed in 1951, except 6000 Jews who chose to remain in the country. They were brutally persecuted dehumanized and imprisoned. By 1974, almost all of the 6,000 Jews were able to leave either illegally or just when the government allowed random visas.

THE REMOVAL OF THE MONARCHY

THE ARMY IS TAKING CONTROL

In 1958 a revolution occurred in Iraq, demanding and declaring the removal of the monarchy, led by Abd-al- Karim Qasim, a high-ranking army officer. Iraq was proclaimed a Republic. Qasim formed a cabinet and appointed himself commander of the National Force and his aide, General Arif, became Minister of the Interior and Deputy Commander of the Armed Forces. Instability between Qasim and Arif quickly escalated. One faction of the army with the Arab Nationalist group rebelled against Qasim and his supporters. In 1963 Qasim was executed in a coup lead by Arif. In1966 Arif died in a helicopter accident and his brother assumed power.

In 1968 came the rise of the **socialist Baath party.**

On March 20, 2003 Sadam Hussain's regime was put down, by the United States and its Allied, in an invasion known as Operation Iraqi Freedom.

The Murad family experienced a difficult life in Iraq. It was not a comfortable place for a Jewish community and our belief system was challenged time and time again. As we developed and matured, so did the hatred aimed towards us. We called Iraq home, but it never felt the way a home should feel. There was love within the walls of our home, but abhorrence outside of it. We looked around and saw so few that shared our beliefs. Often times, we felt like we were trapped on an island with only one another to rely upon.

With these feelings at the forefront of our lives, we collectively decided there was a better place for us; a place to rebuild and recast our nets; a place we could not only call home, but also feel as if we were home. This desire for acceptance and comfort led us back to our heritage, to our holy land, and to our people's beginning--Israel.

Part III

The Journey

Adieu, Babylon. . .It may be gone, Yet the legacy lives on, Here's the story of Babel, We live to tell.

My family's journey from Iraq to Israel was not easy; there were many dangers to overcome, and emotions ran high, but we learned a lot of valuable lessons, and grew stronger as a family.

This is the story of the Murad family's escape from where our ancestors lived continuously for almost 2600 years. The escape was not easy. A lot of suffering and dislocation followed during the last few years of our stay in that land, and the relocation and adjustment in the new land, Israel, was challenging.

Still, other nationalities and minorities that lived in Babylon for over 2600 years were not so lucky. Their descendants are still suffering persecution and humiliation to this very day. Nations and remnants of nations, such as, Chaldeans, Assyrians, and Armenians still live in Iraq. They still speak their historic languages, have their own Christian Churches and keep their own customs; but their numbers are dwindling fast because of the persecution, humiliation and lack of opportunities.

THE ZIONIST MOVEMENT IN IRAQ

It was 1948, just after Israel declared its independence, and sentiment for Israel ran high among all Jews in Iraq, especially among the youth. None of us had any future in Iraq, and so we joined the "Movement" (Tnu'a). We met in small groups once a week, and our link was the "Guide" (Madrikh), usually one of our friends, who had been in the Movement longer than us, graduated from its classes, and gained fluency in Hebrew. As we grew up, we all had basic training in Hebrew at the Midrash (school), but we needed to learn Modern Hebrew and its handwriting. We practiced mastering the language during those weekly meetings, and also heard news about Israel, learned the history of the Zionist Movement, and discussed the situation of the Jews in Iraq. But really we were doing much more than just that: We were preparing for immigration to Israel.

On one occasion, we were briefed about a visit by the emissary, called in Hebrew *Shaliakh,* sent by the Jewish Agency to oversee this activity. The emissary had a first name only; he did not know Arabic and spoke only Hebrew. Of course, it was all underground, secretive, and hidden from the eyes of the authorities. But they knew, and they followed us. The Iraqi Government knew everything and tolerated it, and actually encouraged it, because they had a plan that would unfold in stages.

At first, they started with restrictions in business. Next was a law that required all Jewish businesses to have a Muslim partner. Those Muslims first needed to learn about how to manage a business, and then, when the time came, they would take over when we all left Iraq. Then a law was passed allowing all Jews to renounce their Iraqi citizenship. Most Jews took advantage of the law and were even encouraged by the authorities. The younger generation, myself (Aaron) included, worked for a few months in an office set up especially for Jews to fill out the forms needed to renounce their

Iraqi citizenship. I interviewed each person separately, and got all the details needed to fill in the applications. I processed hundreds of those forms every day, and by the end of that 3-4 month period, I filled out thousands and thousands of applications. This was not done for money, and was fueled by passion.

One day, at an important meeting in our house, the Emissary was present; he gave a speech, answered questions, and participated in discussions. There were about 20 young men and women present. Suddenly there was a knock on the door. We were all seated in our living room, and when the door opened, all those present would clearly be seen. And who was standing at the doorsill? There were four young Muslim men in suits, who peered inside immediately, then recoiled, as if they had made a mistake. They were from the Iraqi Secret Police, and had been following us. "That's OK," one of them said. "We made a mistake. Thank you."

They saw what he needed to see, and then they all left. Everybody knew that we had been followed. But strangely, nothing happened afterward, nothing at all. All they needed was to confirm our presence. And they knew exactly what we were doing.

One day, after deliberations with my parents, we were given permission to build a secret compartment inside the floor in our house. This compartment was to contain Hebrew books of study, but more importantly, if need be, it could be used to store guns and explosives for self-defense. Never again would there be another Farhoud (Pogrom), or wave of bloodletting without self-defense.

And so, a guy came at an appointed hour and built the compartment. It was a professional job, the compartment could be opened at will, but its opening could not be seen, even to the trained eye. Fortunately, we only ever needed to store Hebrew books and notebooks. Until the day everybody left Iraq, it was not needed for any other purpose.

PREPARATIONS FOR THE ILLEGAL JOURNEY

It was January 1950. The majority of the Iraqi Jews took advantage of the new law to renounce their citizenship, and the process was continuing. No one thought of the possible repercussions. We had a state to go to, the State of Israel. We did not mind being temporarily stateless refugees, but we came to find out it was for much longer than anticipated. The Iraqi Government had plans for us: They would, in time, confiscate all properties belonging to us, our businesses, stocks of merchandise, homes, money, basically everything.

Our transportation to Israel was going very slowly. It was estimated that it would take several years to transport the estimated 120,000-150,000 Jews from Iraq to the new homeland. Therefore, a number of youths decided to take a path of crossing the borders illegally. Immigration from Tehran was going much faster than from Baghdad. It is estimated that about twenty-five thousand youth immigrated illegally.

Those who aided in the smuggling were prominent members of the Muslim society, and had contacts everywhere. They did not negotiate directly, but had agents who did the job for them, agents in the Jewish society itself. All the while, the authorities colluded for some share, looked the other way, or tacitly agreed to help.

Some operatives were not so good. For instance, three Jewish youths found some people to transport them across the border who had an original idea of how to do it undetected, right under the nose of the authorities. These people put the three poor guys in the back of an insulated ice truck, and then filled the front space with a truck-full of ice. And on they went for a long journey. If there was an inspection by authorities, they planned to open the back door of the truck and show that it was full of ice. When they approached the border, they let the men out so they could make the last trek on foot, but instead found them frozen to death. In their stupidity, they put them out under the scorching sun to thaw, in the hope they would rise and make the walk. The three poor guys were frozen and long gone, and of course did not revive.

MY OWN ILLEGAL JOURNEY

As a young man already associated with the movement, it was decided that I would make the illegal journey to Israel. I was to travel with friends, and would later be joined by the rest of my family.

About a week after my father paid the fee to the agents who set up my journey, the word came, "Get ready to go." They specified a day, which fell the week after. We were all joyful that the trip could begin and that I would be in Israel very soon. No one dreamed that it was to be a much longer wait.

"Aaron, my son" said my father, which was how he always addressed me. "Here we have two gold and diamond rings belonging to your mother. Take them with you. Take care of them, and if you need them to help you in an emergency, use them."

When the time came, I was ready with a small "biqcha", which is a square piece of cloth tied together with its four corners. The two valuable rings were hooked with a safety pin on the inside of my underwear. I went with them, and slept with them all the time. I was instructed never to mention them or show them to anyone. During the trip, I always felt them whenever I could to make sure that they were still there.

On the appointed day, well after dark, a car stopped near the door of our house and I stood up, said a quick goodbye to my parents, brothers and sisters, and left. I did not expect a dramatic and sad event to happen in my absence. With me in the car, as expected, were the two friends who were scheduled to accompany me on the journey.

They drove us for a few hours in the dark of the night, after which we reached a large estate situated somewhere in a desert looking, flat terrain. The driver and his companion took us inside to a spacious living room, full of Persian carpets and high quality furniture. They quickly brought in lightweight mattresses, which were laid on the carpets, and we slept for what we thought would be just overnight.

We stayed in that living room for over two weeks. I was waiting for a signal to begin my trip, but only my two young friends were permitted to leave; they were eventually replaced by two older men in their early forties, with whom the rest of the trip was made. Our needs were well taken care of during our stay; a young man in his early twenties served us food and drink. He was the son of the owner, and occasionally played backgammon with us, but the two-week stay was too long for me. I wanted it to be over with, to cross the border to Iran and then onwards to Israel.

Nevertheless, I had time to reflect. I wondered why I was doing this--why all the Iraqi Jews were taking this journey. We were all well established and relatively comfortable, except for the incessant persecution. Yet we were born into it, and grew up surrounded by these Muslims, Shia or Sunni, so why run?

The Jewish community was well organized, and numbered about 130,000 in Baghdad, alone. We had our own schools, religious courts, and places of business. Why would a people so well organized, so long established, want to leave en masse, voluntarily and suddenly after 2,600 years?

Persecution was everywhere, practiced both by the state and by individuals. You had to expect a lower status. And we lived under a constant shadow of attack. Discrimination was rampant. It was an accepted way of life.

These were memories that occurred to me when I was confined to that huge estate, just waiting and waiting.

ON THE ROAD

After two weeks, the word finally came that we were to leave the next day. I was glad to exit that big estate, where we were confined to the living room. Even to go to the bathroom, we had to get permission first, and before permitting us, they would alert their women to hide from our faces, lest we have a glimpse of them.

It was early in the morning, almost before the sun came out, when a car stopped by and we all huddled in to our seats. There was the driver and one more person, possibly a guide. By late afternoon, well before dusk, we could see a huge Bedouin encampment of a few thousand huts in the distance. Historically the Bedouins used goat hair to weave the cloth of their tents, and their own clothes, but over time they switched to manufactured black thread. They wove their cloth with wooden homemade equipment, a process that was lengthy, but at the end of a day's work, they made a good and strong piece of cloth.

As we drove into the encampment, we were suddenly surrounded by lots of tents, Bedouins on foot, and a lot of livestock, such as goats, sheep and, of course, horses. We kept driving till we reached a judge tent situated in the middle of the encampment. We got off, and were led inside; it was like a big room in a modern house, with carpets covering the floors. We were lead to a corner of the tent and sat down on the floor. I thought this must be the tent of an important person, maybe the Sheikh (Chief) of the tribe!! And as it turns out, I was right!

That night was a special occasion for the Sheikh and his entourage. They had some VIP persons coming for a visit, and we were invited to the occasion too, since we were there and had to spend the night in that big tent. There was a lot of activity and preparations. Some men slaughtered a sheep for the occasion, prepared it, made a huge fire, and then barbequed it, while some women prepared and cooked a lot of rice and other side dishes. Everything was laid nicely in the middle of the tent on huge, metal plates known as *sinniyi*. The sight and smell of the food was very inviting.

Late in the evening, the guests began to arrive, and then the Sheikh came in, clad with his Arab headdress and *Abaya*. One of the assistants turned to us and said calmly, "*This is our Sheikh.*" Everyone sat with their legs crossed. We waited for them to start eating, and as one put forward his arm, we did so too. We all ate using our fingers to grab the rice, or cut a piece of the meat. Each person formed a large ball-shaped, mouthful of rice, then put it into his mouth to eat. We knew that was their custom and we did the same with acceptance and respect for that tradition. Ooks were already preparing black Arabian coffee, which they later served in very small cups. The brewed coffee was prepared in special brass jugs, and was filtered as they poured by a brush-like contraption conveniently stationed at the end of the spout.

All was well. Discussions were made and when it was time to sleep, the guests left with a lot of hugs with the Sheikh and his aides. They removed the remnants of the food, and the place quickly became clean and orderly. Other assistants brought in a metal bed, and prepared it for the Sheikh. The bed was not something to brag about, but he was the only one to sleep on a bed. All the rest of us slept on mattresses set on the floor. I slept the rest of the night, not fearing anything.

I was awakened by sounds of sheep and goats being driven out to pasture. The sun was dawning, and I was excited for what lay ahead. We were supposed to cross the border to Iran that day. After awaking, we were given a breakfast of bread, goat milk, goat cheese, and eggs. The bread was baked before our eyes in large, baked mud oven called *tannur.* The women flattened pieces of dough then stuck them inside the oven. The fire burned from dry shrubs and sun-dried animal excrement. The women collectedthe dry shrubs from the wilderness, and then put them in a sack, which they put on their back and hung around their neck. While out collecting dry shrubs, they also collected the animal excrement, which they flattened and put in the sun to dry. Later they would use it as fuel for open fire, in sun-dried mud ovens. The piece of bread was ready in minutes. The women dipped their hands into those burning ovens and took out the pieces that were ready, and replaced them with fresh pieces of flattened dough.

The car was ready within a short time and the driver came to pick us up. He was accompanied by the guide, who sat near him in the front seat, while the three of us sat in the back. We drove for about two hours, and suddenly saw a river. The water was muddy, shallow, and there were a lot of trees, in contrast to the flat terrain we left earlier. This was one of the tributaries of the Tigris River, one of the two great lifelines of Iraq that straddled the country from north to south and down into the Persian Gulf. Together with the Euphrates, the Tigris made Iraq one of the most fertile areas of the world, and the rivers are the reason it became known as "the cradle of civilization."

Our car stopped just before the water, and a lot of Bedouins came running over. After a little confusion, a few men came to us, turned around, kneeled on the floor, and motioned us to ride on their backs. "We will take you to the other side of the river" one of them said to us. So we climbed on and they stood up and started walking towards the river. The water was muddy, but flowing. You could not see through it. The waded into the water, and at the deepest point it was waist high, but they crossed with ease and reached the other shore within minutes. They let us down, and then went back into the water to get back to the other side.

But what about the car? How is it going to cross the river? We thought. There was a discussion on the opposite shore, but within a few moments the driver got into the car with his guide and one of the Bedouins and they sped along the river. The car went into the distance and became gradually smaller to our eyes until we could not see it anymore. Did they run away from us? No. About 30 minutes later, we saw the car coming towards us from the distance, and it was definitely on our side of the river. They reached us and stopped. The Bedouin they had taken along was a guide who knew of shallow places in the river just a few miles away. There the car crossed the river with the wheels only half submerged in the water. A clean crossing! Soon the Bedouin guide got out of the car, we got in, and on we went.

Within a short drive, we started to see the mountain range ahead of us. Another hour's drive and we were at the foot of the mountain. The car stopped, it could not go any further. Then two Kurdish guides took over: "We will now continue our journey on foot," one of them said, "Be ready to cross the mountains."

Really? Cross the mountains on foot? And for how long? We were not prepared to venture into the wild; and those mountains were steep, rocky and barren.

AHMED

"It is not so bad," said one of the guides. "We will be walking for about two hours through the mountains, then we will be near the border. A guy by the name of Ahmed will greet you there, scream his name loudly when you reach the top of the mountain, he will come for you and take you to the border where the Iranian border police will be waiting to take you in," he concluded.

A breath of relief! We would soon be in Iran. And with that news, we started our walk.

And so, I will soon be leaving Iraq, I thought. Babylon of my grandfathers, who lived there for 2600 years. I am leaving without regret, without remorse, looking for a future in the land of Israel, the land of my ancestors. It was time.

After walking and climbing the mountain, we reached the summit, and looked downwards at a deep but clear ravine. Our guide motioned us to stop, and started hollering at the top of his voice: "Ahmed! Ahmed!" and then he showed up, headscarf first. He motioned us to cross the ravine to him. When we reached Ahmed he motioned us to continue walking. It took only 10 minutes, and he said, "This is the border" and we saw people on the other side looking at us, happy and smiling. When we were about 15 feet away, Ahmed said goodbye and motioned us to go greet the Iranian commander and two border police manning the border station. The commander came towards us with hands stretched saying, "Welcome. . .Welcome. . .Welcome to freedom!!!"

IRAN

These were soothing words. We all shook his hand with gratefulness and relief. We were then motioned to come inside the border station, a 2-room built structure with no luxury, but with the Iranian flag flying on top. I should call this border station "the stripping station," where you get stripped of your money, and clothes. We did not believe it was going to happen, but the Commander said it was necessary. It was his job. It was the Law.

We were led to the commander's inner office and were asked to take off our clothes, except for the underwear. They asked if we had any money or other valuables. They believed that I did not have anything, as they saw that I had next to nothing with me. I was a teenager. They did not even want to search me. Of course, I did not mention the rings attached to my underwear. These things did not show, and I got away with it. The two older guys had lots of money, and other valuables. They declared everything. I was motioned to get out of the private room, and what went on inside after was not clear to me, but I know the commander got paid his share.

As soon as we were done, they called a taxi, which took us to the house of the only Jewish family left in the village near that border station. All the other families had already immigrated to Israel. This family was paid to receive all Jewish refugees from Iraq, and give them shelter and food until they were taken by bus to Tehran, where the Jewish Agency had a large refugee Camp.

In our case, it was a little different. As soon as the taxi arrived at the house, the two older guys that traveled with me turned to the house lady and ordered the best foods they could imagine. I suppose they felt comfortable since they were now finished with Iraq and were now free people, in a free country. They forgot that we all were still refugees with no official status, and could be taken advantage of easily.

The lady smelled money. She kept eying us constantly. She forbade us to close the door of our room, keeping us under surveillance, but she prepared everything they requested. Later she told us that her husband went on a business trip to Tehran and would be back within a few days. We had to wait for him; otherwise we were not free to go.

When the guy did come back four days later, I got a little surprise. It was shocking to see him being treated by his wife and several children, not only like a king, but also more importantly, like their Master. In the Iranian language, the word master translates into the word "*Agha.*" So when he appeared at the doorsill, his entire family all stood up and bowed down to him, saying in a loud voice, "Agha." Then he motioned them to go their ways. He was done. He entered and his obedient wife served him food. They talked as he ate his mouthfuls.

Later, he came to our room, sat down with the two older guys and did his 'accounting.' He charged us lots of money for the four days we all stayed at his house, which means he was paid double since he also got money from the Jewish Agency for every Jew coming as a refugee to his house. After receiving his payment, he promised to take us the next day to the station, where a bus was scheduled to make the trip to Tehran.

Next morning, at the early hour of 6:00 a.m., on rolled the bus to Tehran, full of passengers and baggage. It was a serious distance between the border village and Tehran. It took about eight hours with stops. We passed through many cities and villages. The scenery was totally different from what I was used to in Iraq, or Lebanon, or any other Arab country. The environment, the trees, the mountains, the deserts, the snow, the way people talked, and the revered authority were all different. The impression was that this country was run efficiently, and had potential. Things moved; there was a directing hand.

Late in the evening, the bus arrived at the Collection Camp in Tehran. We got out of the bus and were immediately shown into one of the small one-room structures. We were assigned beds, given some sandwiches and water, and left alone to rest from the trip. My two older friends took a taxi to somewhere they knew in Tehran, and I never saw or heard of them again.

Now I was free. I was in the Jewish Agency's Camp, and I expected to be in Israel within a week or so; but again, it was to take much longer than I expected.

It had been over four weeks since had I left home in Baghdad, and things had changed. Israel, at that time, had a few old turbine airplanes that they used to transport hundreds of thousands immigrants, or "Olim" across the border. They had whole communities from all over Europe, Yemen, Iraq, Iran, North Africa, and other parts of the world who were ready and packed to come to Israel immediately and realize a dream of centuries—to live in the Promised Land.

It was a miracle that no accidents occurred; that no plane fell from the sky, and all those hundreds of thousands of people were actually transported by these old airplanes, all safely and securely.

Because of political pressure, and the fact that all the Iraqi Jews had renounced their citizenship and were practically sitting on luggage and waiting to leave, Israel diverted its flying machines to get the Iraqi Jews to Israel. Therefore, those of us in the collection camp in Tehran were left to wait. Very few flights left Tehran and we were there for a few months. Life at the camp was not so bad. There was no lack of food, but we had to cook, and care for all our own needs.

One day, I had a surprise. Who did I meet in the camp? My cousin and friend, Edmond Es'haik. "My dear fellow, my cousin, how are you, and when did you arrive?" I said.

"I just arrived," he answered. And we sat chatting and telling each other our experiences. My cousin and I stayed together in the same room; we helped each other, and waited for the trip to end. So many youth followed this route of crossing the border to Tehran, and then to Israel.

Finally, the day arrived; a flight was ready to take us. That evening a bus took us to the airport, and we went up in the airplane. It flew directly to Israel. It was a night flight, probably on purpose because we crossed over Iraq and Jordan. During that flight, which took several hours, I felt extreme happiness that my ordeal would finally come to an end.

The airplane was so old that fissures between the metal parts were allowing outside air to come in and pieces of metal on the body were shaking with the wind. We were all huddled in the airplane, many of us sitting on the floor for lack of seats, and as I said, it was a miracle that no accident happened. The plane was flying very low to avoid detection through its flight over Iraq and Jordan. It carried us to the Lod airport in Israel. Today this airport is called "Ben Gurion International Airport:" The main airport of Israel.

We arrived in the middle of the night. It was dark; it was silent; the smell of orange groves was all around. It was the smell of roses for us, the smell of pure air, of freedom.

Preparations of the Murad Family for Immigration

ORIT'S RECOLLECTIONS AND STORIES

The Iraqi authorities allowed the Jews to take only one suitcase per person. Obviously, it was difficult to decide what to fit in one suitcase, and heads were spinning, or maybe the world around them was spinning.

This hasty departure from Iraq was actually much like the exodus of the Jews from Egypt, thousands of years earlier. Everyone left in a haste to get rid of slavery and welcome freedom. In this transition period, the community was in a state of readiness, they took matters seriously, as fast action and huge sacrifices were necessary to obtain their freedom.

To uproot an affluent and well-established community created a certain degree of uproar. All houses contained quality Persian carpets, expensive furniture, gold, silver, and other valuables. Could we fit our pillows, comforters, sheets and towels in one suitcase? No, instead they were sold at a much-reduced price to the Arabs.

Nobody knew exactly what to expect in this huge confusion. Jews needed each other's support; they got information and tips at meeting places such as the "Qahua" (coffee shop) or the Souk (market) and the synagogues. That is where you could feel the community's pulse; its fear and anxiety caused by the presence of danger; its agitation, uneasiness or apprehensiveness, caused by their uncertain status.

Additional woes were created by random government announcements that threatened severe punishment to anyone caught contravening their guidelines. It was also warned that government employees would thoroughly inspect all suitcases and would remove any suspicious items, which could result in people's arrests. The Jews indeed had a reasons to be extraordinarily fearful.

In the central market of Baghdad it was chaos. It became unusually crowded with Jews pushing against each other in an attempt to buy suitcases or other necessities for the big departure. Everyone wanted a last glimpse of the Shorga (the Jewish market), a last walk on the familiar streets, a last look at houses and businesses. People pushed and banged their elbows against each other, saying, "Move this way" or "Let me get out of here, I can't breathe anymore" or "Stop shouting, will you?"

Dresses were one of my favorite. I always wore nice dresses and when my mother suddenly told me to go with her to get some more dresses for our departure, I was extra happy knowing that one of those dresses would be red. My mother thought that red was the best color on me.

I would have to wear the dresses one on top of the other on our way to the airport. My mother said everybody was going to do that, but I kept thinking it was going to get so hot on the airplane. How exciting-- Israel, we would have to speak only Hebrew. I wished I could speak Hebrew already. Maybe someone would plant this language in me so I didn't have to make the effort to learn. Oh, my cousin, Shoshana, was so lucky her number had arrived already; she would be leaving very soon, even before me.

My father and I went together to bid farewell to my Aunt Muzli, his sister, and I said "Oh, look Papa, they are already on the bus going to the airport." Papa reached the bus in a hurry to greet his sister. Aunt Muzli said, "Come, my brother, I want to kiss you goodbye," my father just motioned with his hands and said, "Oh, its ok, yalla hai heey (never mind)."

It was sad departing from my cousin Shoshana, wondering if we were going to see or play with each other again. The next day, when my father looked on the departure sheet he happily announced that our name and number were on the list. We had one month to prepare and get ready for the big day.

MY FATHER'S TRAGEDY

My father, as usual, always discussed business matters with his father Abi (Menashe). This time the discussion was serious, because the government was moving fast to take over Jewish businesses. Their decision was that maybe my father could go to the office and rescue some of the large amounts of cash kept in the huge safe in the office.

My father agreed to go, in spite of the danger involved. He knew that if he got caught he would immediately go to jail and face death. Nevertheless, he gathered all his courage, and went. While he was inside the office, he heard police steps approaching. He was able to take money and hide it in his shoes. He then rushed out, and luckily the police did not notice him, for otherwise he would have been tortured to death.

The impact was enormous. On his way back home, his entire body was shivering and upon his arrival he said to my mother "Abdalek, I don't know what is going on with me." And right away he started vomiting. Vomiting? What was he vomiting? He was vomiting blood, a lot of it--red, thick blood. I could see my father vomiting in the room, filling it with blood. You could swim in that pool of blood. My mother, all confused, urgently sent my brother to ask her family for help.

My cousin, Dr. Rachamin Elias, arrived to check my father and he diagnosed his situation as an open ulcer and recommended that he should lie in bed and not move at all, so his wound could heal. The bleeding stopped for a while, the room was cleaned, but the family decided to take my father to the hospital.

The news about my father's illness spread like a hurricane, like a 140 mph wind. Everyone in the community heard the horrifying news.

For me, this was like a horror movie; it didn't seem real. *"Maybe it is just a dream,* I thought, watching all this drama take place right in my own house. *Is it really happening to my own father and mother? Is it really happening to my whole family? In front of my own two eyes. It is probably not a dream. . .*

Before leaving for the hospital, my mother wrote the hospital's phone number on a piece of paper and said, "Call me at this number. Go to our neighbor and phone from there."

I followed the family outside the house, standing away from them and watching my father, who was very alert and watching me in return as if he wanted to say," Please be a good girl, please don't get into trouble."

For a little while, I was happy to play with my cousin and my brother, and then I went inside the house in one of the big rooms and thought to myself that when my father was dismissed from the hospital and came home, he would be able to tell us the story of when he was sick and bleeding. But then, I had doubts and felt that maybe this would never happen. Maybe my father would never be able to tell his story in his own words, and then I remembered my father's reaction when I had an urgent question and asked him: "What if someone does not make it to Israel?" he was slightly annoyed and answered, "pity on such a person, that is his bad luck".

I remembered to call my family the next day. I asked the nurse to speak with my mother, but her reply was suspicious and she said that everyone had left the room; she refused to give any more details. It was clear to me that something terrible had happened. The three of us kept quiet and left the neighbor's house. From our reaction the neighbors quickly realized there was bad news because I was already crying, and when we arrived home my sister was on the porch crying, and then it was clear that my father was no longer with us.

Later, I heard that my uncle Albert reported to my father just before he passed, the news that had just come in: Aaron, who was sent illegally to Israel, had just arrived safely. My father was very happy. In a gesture of thanking God, he kissed his hand and put it on his eyes.

We sat Shivaa at my grandfather Menashe's house. My mother sat on a pillow on the floor; mourning the sad and tragic loss of our father.

GET READY TO PACK

Before embarking on our final journey, we had to determine the right luggage to buy that was adequate for our needs. My mother asked my brother-in-law, Meir, if she could join him while he was looking for suitcases. Meir chose to look at *souk l'sfafir,* the Jewish market, and so my mother and I met him there to shop. Walking with Meir was awkward, my smaller footsteps did not match his bigger footsteps and I had to run to catch up with him, like dancing the step dance. It was an everlasting and tiring walk, until Meir finally found someone who carried suitcases. The two big suitcases that Meir bought had to fit inside the Arabbana (horse carriage) that he had hired to take us back home.

Many stories would reach us as to how people were trying to conceal valuables or money from the eyes of the authorities. Some people would hide their valuables inside pieces of soap by digging holes inside the soap, then closing the hole and putting the soap back in its original package. Some would also hide things inside shaving brushes, and others went as far as swallowing diamond rings. Various people chose to hide those last precious valuables inside their shoes or shoe heals, or inside suitcase linings. People came up with numerous ideas when they had to play hide and seek with the Iraqi government.

AT THE AIRPORT IN BAGHDAD

Two weeks later, on route to the airport, we took the same bus that my Aunt Muzli had taken when we bid her goodbye. Ready, set, go! The government bus drove us along, and each one of us were wearing layers of clothes that we would never end up using in Israel anyway.

The same people who scared my father to death inspected us. Now I was scared to death. My anticipation to go to Israel was as real as my father's death, only that now it was without him, and instead with five dresses worn one on top of each other, one of which was red.

My small gold earrings happened to remain on my ears. At the airport, a woman inspected those tiny earrings thoroughly, until my mother assured her that they were tiny and worth next to nothing. I was still petrified from the thought that I might have to stay in Baghdad by myself and my family would leave without me for Israel. The inspector was finally convinced that my tiny earring had almost no value, and allowed us to board the plane.

ON THE EAGLE'S WINGS - FROM BAGHDAD TO TEL- AVIV

It was 1950 and the mass immigration to Israel was already underway. Many families owned Torah Scrolls that were being used in the synagogues. The Torah Scrolls were very dear to the families involved, and they would not give them up. Many of them decided to bring the Scrolls along on the same airplane they were boarding. Thus, hundred of precious Torahs, written by dedicated and famous Iraqi Scribes, arrived in Israel.

Grandfather Menashe did the same. He took his two Torahs with him to the airport of Baghdad and instructed Arab employees at the airport to take good care of the Scrolls, because they were Holy. Moreover, he intimidated the employees and said, "Anyone who handles them roughly, would be punished in heaven."

A JOURNEY WORTH MAKING

Our family's journey to the Promised Land was difficult and full of tragedy, but all the hardships were worth it once we arrived home in Israel. We lived and experienced first hand one of the most amazing immigration stories known to man, and it is a blessing to be able to share our incredible journey with present and future generations. We hope the story of our journey will inspire others to look inside and seek the courage to travel to where they truly belong.

Part IV
The Destination

"To bring about the unconditional love,
We must release the past and forgive."

—Rambam

ISRAEL

We were all huddled on a lorry, with no seats, and no comfort, like sheep being transported; but we were happy that the ordeal was over, and more importantly, happy that we were in Israel. The lorry took us to Haifa, where the great immigration camp, "Sha'ar Ha'Aliyah" was stationed.

CONFUSION IN NAMES

When Aaron Murad was asked to give his second name at the immigration counter in Israel he was confused.

In Iraq, we occasionally gave the family name by which the family's grandfather or in our case our great grandfather was known, "Hackam-David." When translated into Arabic the name would be "Mouallem- David," but by mistake they wrote simply "Mouallem". In the end, we reported three family names: When our mother finally arrived she gave the name "Hacham- David", where as our brother Moshe used "Murad," and Aaron used "Mouallem"!!! Later we unified the names and decided on a more Hebrew-sounding one, "Ben- Mordechai."

At the Camp of Sha'ar Ha'Aliyah, following the registration, we were given sandwiches to eat made of black bread and jam. We devoured these, and immediately wanted more!! Finally, we were shown beds in a large tent. According to Aaron's recollection he could see a great encampment stretching far into the distance.

The next day Aaron took the bus straight to Tel Aviv to try and find relatives, friends, and possibly a job. Whom did he meet? No other than Mr. Meir Yechezkiel Murad, accompanied by his eldest son, Salim. Meir Murad was my aunt's husband, and cousin to both our parents, and an important player in the Murad family. He was a very successful businessman back in Iraq. His huge business was confiscated, of course, like all the others, but he still had his investments, securities, and money well kept in British and European banks: He was in good shape. We talked about the immigration process but by then I (Aaron) knew that all the Jews of Iraq were going to end up in Israel within the coming few weeks, so felt confident I would see my family soon. During our conversation he mentioned something that made me suspicious something unhappy had happened back in Iraq, and it was clear he did not want to talk for long.

Although, they were both very anxious to see me, talk to me, observe my reaction to things. They both admired me, which was complimentary because I admired them too, especially, the father, Meir. He was a hero to me. Even my father, who was a deep thinker, admired his intellect and deep understanding. That day, I went back to Sha'ar Ha'Aliyah in Haifa suspicious and doubtful, but still happy I did not hear something bad.

A few days later, I was walking in the Camp and suddenly spotted my dear uncle Albert. His appearance and demeanor were not encouraging. I looked at him and saw what I was dreading: He was wearing a black tie, the sign of mourning. I stared at him straight in the eye and he said slowly, "your father" and stopped. I understood at that moment that my father had passed away back in Iraq. He did not have the chance to see the Promised Land. He cherished it and he wanted to come, but G-d planned otherwise.

I hugged my uncle Albert, crying. He was very supportive and said all the soothing words that I needed, but he was just as sad as I was and he needed support as much as I did. I also learned that my brother, Moshe had already come to Israel, he came by himself and did not wait for everyone in the family. He did not know, his flight was before the sad event, and therefore I had the duty to find where he was sent by the management of the Camp, to meet him, and give him the bad news about our father.

The next day, I went to the management office to find out where he was placed. He was sent south of Tel Aviv, to Gedera, a village known to be full of new immigrants. I took the bus and immediately went south to Gedera. When I finally reached that village, it was not difficult to find him. He had a tent all by himself and surrounding his tent were many other new immigrants in tents fixed on the sandy ground. All they had was shelter, and sandy earth; but they were happy to be home. Reluctantly I told my brother of our father's death, and we mourned him together.

INNER STRENGTH

The bittersweet immigration to Israel after my father's sudden death was not easy for my mother. The sudden hurdle of packing in just one suitcase per person was confusing and beyond her ability. What should she pack? What about her beautiful personal jewelry? What about the furniture and household items? Should she quickly sell them? Where should she put the religious items her father, Rabbi Ezra, wrote and dedicated to her? She had a huge collection of Shabbat and Holiday chinaware and silverware that she had accumulated throughout the years: Where would she keep them? What should she do with her abundance of gold gathered inside two huge garbage bags? Gold for her children's birth, gold to beautify the hair, gold hands against the evil eye, gold hegel (baby anklets) and so much more!! To accomplish her mission, she needed all her strength. She needed to gather a phenomenon called *inner strength*.

Gathering inner strength is an exploration to find your authentic self, an effort to dig inside yourself to bring about a strength, which at times, we do not think we possess. She had a great desire to use her inner powers to deal with the mass exodus from one country to another; she had to follow the saying, "Do not let what you cannot do interfere with what you can do."

My mother had an urgent responsibility in an urgent situation amidst her personal chaos. She had the power and strength to question the details of her husband's death and demanded answers. She faced these difficulties with the power to judge what was more important than her needs. She considered her family's needs above her own, and moved forward with a powerful positive attitude, faith, and strength.

ARRIVING IN ISRAEL

The first people boarding the plane were able to get a seat; others had to stand holding a bar for support. It was hot on the plane, especially when we all were wearing layers of clothes, and when we finally landed, people wanted to get out at the same time, creating chaos. I was in the middle of an older group of people, squished and barely able to breathe. I lifted my head to get some air, worried about what I should do if I did not find my family. My brother, Emile, was already outside the craft, waiting for me. Bothered by my delay he said, "There is a little girl, she is probably squished, can you let her get out?" People listened and let me leave before them, saying, "Go, go," while patting me on my back.

We headed to government counters at the airport in Israel, and lined up for registration. We advanced some more and we noticed one employee holding a big spraying device containing the disinfectant chemical called DDT. He proceeded to spray us and the DDT affected my breathing until I got some fresh air outside the building.

In 1962, the American biologist, Rachel Carson, revealed that the use of DDT was extremely toxic and was impacting both the environment and human health. In 1972 the use of DDT was banned in the United States; and to think, we practically took a shower in the stuff!

At Lydia Airport, we received a light meal, and then we got on big trucks and headed north to Sha'ar Aliyah (absorption camp) where we received medical examinations and were given food stamps. For the next two weeks we lived in this camp sleeping in tents. The tents were huge, containing rows of beds on both sides. We lined up for food, which consisted of bread, margarine, and jam. Two weeks later, the immigrants were transferred to various transition camps (called in Hebrew, Ma'abarot) in different locations all over Israel. My family was transferred to the Ma'abara of Ra'anana located in the area of Hod Hasharon today.

Upon arrival, the Israeli authorities informed all owners that they would store their Scrolls safely in the customs warehouse in Jaffa, and would return them back after the initial settlement of the families in Israel. A short time afterwards, Uncle Jacob and Uncle Isaac heard that a huge fire broke out in the warehouse where the Torahs were stored. Hundreds of precious Torah Scrolls were burnt in this fire. Jacob and Isaac immediately rushed to the warehouse, very concerned, and upon arrival saw a huge crowd of Iraqi Jews looking for their Torahs. Jacob and Isaac diligently searched the warehouse in the hope of finding their Scrolls. Suddenly, they saw them; they were intact and standing side by side as though they were two twin brothers. It was a miracle that the Scrolls survived the fire without any damage, as very few Torahs were recovered.

However, the warehouse owners suddenly claimed any available Torahs, including the two that belonged to Jacob and Isaac. The story goes that one government employee said to Jacob, "I will not permit you to take possession of your Scrolls." This angered Jacob, who asked for an explanation. The employee continued to resist and finally gave an unexpected answer: "Because you are not religious, you are not wearing a kippa." Luckily, a person from the crowd came to Jacob's rescue and handed him a Kippa, which he put on and approached the employee again; only then did the employee allow Jacob to take the Scrolls.

After so many challenges, and miracles, Rabbi Ezra's precious Scrolls survived. These are the only two surviving Scrolls from that generation in Murad family history.

WELCOME TO MA'ABARA STORIES AND EXPERIENCES

There was already a well-established tradition of people immigrating to Israel to escape persecution. In 1882, increased Anti-Semitism in Russia brought the first Aliyah of Biluim. They established the colonies in Gedera, Rishon Le-Zion, and Petach Tikvah; within fifteen years they established eighteen Jewish.

There was no electricity in our tent village, and we often lacked other necessities. My brother Moshe would line up every Friday for *Challa* (Traditional bread for Shabbat), but one Friday he was late. He stood in line, but by the time his turn arrived, the Challas were finished. Moshe decided to ask the neighbor to share some of his Challas, and happily returned to the tent with ten loaves. This abundance made us search for answers all day on Saturday. How did the neighbor have so many extra Challas to spare? Maybe he got double the amount? After Shabbat, Moshe found out that the generous neighbor gave us all of his Challas. Even during hard times, our neighbor gave us all he had to spare.

My mother always warned us about scorpions. "Do not go near the bushes," she would say. Once, when I was looking inside the bush, I saw a big scorpion crawling around. Luckily, I walked away safely. Ironically, a scorpion stung my mother on her finger. She needed immediate treatment, but there was no medical service in the Ma'abara!! She had sharp pain and burning, but no help was to be found, so she treated it herself. She tightly tied the finger with a thin strip of cloth so the poisoned blood would not travel through her veins; then she squeezed the other part of her finger to let the poisoned blood out. The woman, who was accustomed to a luxurious life, was now in a Ma'bara successfully treating her own scorpion bite.

RED BEETS DISH

Uncle Jacob was transferred to Ma'abara Ra'anana. During his first week in the Ma'bara, my mother offered a cooked meal. It was sweet and sour beets with shelled *kubba* (meatballs). My mother asked me to deliver it to my uncle's tent. Beets were not my favorite vegetable; nevertheless, on the way I became curious and opened the hot pot. The smell of the hot beets and shelled kubba shot right up my nose made my mouth water. The beets were blinking to me as if to say, "Do not hesitate, please! I am the apple of the Garden of Eden. . .do not let guilt stop you, go ahead. . .taste me, try me. . .you are surely going to like me. . .this is your only chance to decide my fate. . ." I quickly gave in, and after my "evil" tasting, I realized that beets were delicious after all; especially how my mother cooked them.

REBELLION IN MY TENT

Eight human beings living in one small tent was surely not ideal. At one point in the Ma'abara I developed opposition to authority; it was probably caused by a conflict between my brother and I.

I thought that I was an easygoing person, who could never be angered, but I was wrong. When my older brother shouted at me, I so angry that I have decided to leave the tent and the Maa'bara all together, to go to my Aunt Habiba in Ramat-Gan or to my grandfather Abi in Tel-Mond. I was determined and I left immediately after the fight. I had to walk through the deep hot sand for half an hour, then through the crooked forest path to the Ra'anana, and then I had to take the bus to my Aunt Habiba, where I might be a bit spoiled and loved.

Unfortunately, my memory did not serve me right and I got off the bus one stop before the big round circle across from my Aunt's house and the Elite Chocolate Factory. As soon as I got off I realized the mistake. I asked passersby where the big Kikar (circle) was, but no one knew--if only I had just mentioned the Elite Chocolate factory. Luckily, someone asked, "Where are you from?" and I said that I was from Baghdad, he said, "Come with me."

He brought me to an Iraqi family living in Ramat-Gan. I said to the woman that I was lost, and no one knew where to find the big Kikar. I spent the whole afternoon with this family in their kitchen, the woman served me from the food that she was cooking, and then asked what my father was doing. When I answered, "I have no father" she was tearful and compassionate. I felt very lonely, but still did not desire to go back just yet—I was not done being angry.

The family showed me the way to go back to the Maa'bara. I arrived to Ra'anana at sunset, got off at the right bus stop, and repeated the usual process: cross the twisted forest path, stomp my feet through the deep sand, and walk to the tent. It was an embarrassing and unaccomplished mission. I still yearned to go to my Aunt Habiba's, or to Abi's. I still longed for my father, his protection, and his unconditional love.

Upon reaching the tent, I hesitantly stood outside before making my debut, and over heard my mother blaming my brother for my sudden disappearance. I was pleased to know that my mother was supporting me, and I was relieved that she was happy to see me. When I went inside she said, "Here she is, she is back."

BLINKING CORNFIELDS

Conditions improved after one month in the Maa'bara, the immigrants (Olim) got an undivided mobile home that was used as a bedroom, kitchen, and eating area all in one package. What a change!! Almost too good to be true.

The mobile homes were on the hill where you could view the valley below. In the valley, farmers grew all sorts of vegetables and corn. Bright and flowering green fields of sweet corn, sprinkled with water feeding the soil and fighting hunger. The earth smelled fresh and new, promising warmth. The scenery was amazing; I have never seen such huge fields of corn, which stood in contrast to our underdeveloped area on the hill, surrounded by crowded mobile homes.

Some kids were already making trips to the fields and picking corn, ignoring the rules against such behavior. I followed my spontaneous desire, and decided to join the rest of the kids. Running with them was much like flying with a group of birds trying to reach the fresh and warm soil of the field and pick corn.

We were almost there, almost touching the corn when suddenly, one voice from an unknown kid decided to lead and commanded us to turn back. We were petrified. Kids uttered in frightened voices. . .the guard. . .the guard. . .he is coming. . .holding a gun, pointing it at us. . .he wants to shoot us. . .shoot us. . .the guard. . .he is shooting. . .hurry! The running became a competition; little kids racing, my heart was racing too. . .running as fast as I could to my safe destination on the hill before the guard shot me. All the kids dispersed inside their mobile homes where safety and warmth welcomed them and soothed their fear.

Breathlessly, I sat on the sandy ground by our mobile home. My heart was pounding. Slowly catching my breath, I started thinking, *what if my heart suddenly stopped?* At the same time, I was hoping that my mother would not discover me in this grave situation. When my pulse relaxed and my heartbeat slowed down, I thanked G-d that nobody fired at me.

I dared once more to look at the guard in the valley and was surprised that there were still some more kids in the field, petrified from the guard's rifle, running back as fast as they could to their mobile homes, to their safety. What surprised me even more was that the guard was holding a long stick that looked exactly like a rifle. He pointed it toward the kids as if he was really firing. It is funny what the imagination can create in times of fear.

Temptation can excite and allure, but it is the feeling of emptiness that brings about the temptation. Temptation blocks self-control, and it can be dangerous.

NEW LIFE IN RAMAT-GAN

We remained in the mobile home for about three or four months while my mother and brothers were looking to buy an apartment in Ramat-Gan, where almost all the Iraqi immigrants landed. They found an apartment that was a little bigger than the mobile home, divided into two rooms, with a nice size entrance that served both as a bedroom and the front door. There was one powder room, and a small kitchen with a small balcony all this size of apartment was to accommodate at least six people. The apartment was located on the third floor, and of course, there was no elevator. The big containers of garbage were downstairs. Laundry had to go to the Laundromat, and yet, we considered ourselves tremendously lucky to get our own place where we could finally start a normal life under normal conditions. Aaron and Emile furnished the apartment; the beds were still borrowed from the Jewish Agency and the feathered pillows became a fantastic home for dust mites, those tiny creatures that nest in pillows and bedding thriving on human skin, causing non-stop itchiness all over your body, all around the clock, especially during the night.

We were six people in that apartment. Flora, who lived in Neve Neeman located in the region of Hod Hasharon, would often visit with her daughter Lili. We had six human demands, six personalities, six possibilities, and with Flora and Lili it became eight.

The weather was very humid, and caused many, including myself, to develop asthma. The humid weather was unbearable for asthma; however, our buds flowered. We became stronger everyday and we grew methodically, building on our strong foundation with proper education, happy and sad moments, and whatever life brought along its shores. Each day, brought new challenges, each day we discovered the core strength within ourselves so we could continue to survive, prevail, and achieve our dreams.

ALWAYS THINK BIG

The period of thinking big began when real life started in Ramat-Gan. Unemployment was high, jobs were scarce, but the Olim's ambitions, strong willpower, command in languages, and perseverance helped them acquire jobs in Tel-Aviv.

We arrived after school had already begun, and I joined the class to fight my battles on my own. I faced what was to come and regardless of the possible hardships, I aimed to achieve.

My brother Emile took me to register at Hagiva'a Elementary School in Ramat-Gan. The principal at the school inquired about my first name, and Emile said, "Claire." The principal asked, "What does it mean?" Emile pointed at the ceiling light and said, "It means 'light' in French." The principal said, "It is 'Or' in Hebrew, and for the feminine, it is 'Orit'."

So, I was given the name "Orit." I was the only girl at school called "Orit." A new name, a new luck, and a new status for new immigrant girl from Baghdad.

The Impact of Freedom

What amazed me, as 10-year old girl, was the feeling of freedom. Now I was able to act and live as I chose, without restraints or restrictions. In Iraq, girls were not permitted the same freedoms as boys, but in Israel, I had the right to speak up freely without fear of blemishing my name. I had no interference from uncles, grandfathers, or anyone who thought that he was in control. I had the right to express my opinion and develop my own way of thinking.

I experienced this freedom for the first time when I was wearing my khaki shorts in Ra'anana. It was a striking personal freedom. I felt just like a flying bird in the beautiful, clear blue sky.

At school, my personal freedom expanded to greater levels, and combined with growth and maturity. Learning from new friends and enriching my horizons, I made it a personal goal to become more cultured and open to my surroundings. I already considered myself a very tolerant and accepting person. I enjoyed being amongst friends and I was known to have leadership qualities. I did what any girl looking for new opportunities might have done to advance herself.

One of the things I loved was learning about art, ballet, and music. I discovered that I loved singing and was actually good! Years later, I was able to use my love of singing at a school in Montreal where I used music as a tool to teach elementary students.

I decided to teach myself everything, and independently I learned how to set good examples, use common sense to be polite and considerate, and instilled in myself sage sayings and words of wisdom. Since I lost my father, I had to make it on my own. I had great willpower to propel towards success and achievements, a power that pushed me into action in every area of life. I developed the ability to make my own decisions and I was sure that I could overcome fear, low self-esteem, and endure opposition and hardship in order to facilitate development and growth of my personality. I loved inspiring other people and helped them erase their fear, negativity, and low-self esteem.

MY FIRST PURIM IN 1953

Purim is about the triumph of good against evil. At Hagiva'a Elementary School, in third grade, we celebrated Purim, read the Megilah, sang Purim songs, and dressed up for a Purim competition.

I had no clue what character to be for Purim. It would have been embarrassing just to show up with my regular, day-to-day clothes. On my way to school I decided to visit my aunt Rena. Not knowing what to wear for Purim was annoying, but Rena was there to help. As soon as she heard about the competition, she had an idea. She ran around the house looking for sheets, pajama pants, scarves, soft material for belts, and other fabrics in different colors. I did not know what she was up to and just waited to see the results. She covered me with sheets and tied a wide fabric around my waist, and then she tied a scarf around my neck and covered my hair with different layered fabrics. She said, "Now you are dressed as a Kurdish girl".

A Kurdish girl— Is that what I was? It could be interesting, and I was grateful that at least I was dressed up like everyone else in class; and I admired my aunt's willingness and ideas.

At school, everyone was supposed to introduce their outfits, many students were dressed as figures from the story of Purim, others were dressed up as old men holding a cane, or old women, or even funny figures. The only odd outfit was mine. Although I loved it, I was not sure that my classmates would know the meaning of word "Kurdish."

When my turn arrived to introduce my outfit, I rushed toward the center of the class and said, "I am Kurdish." The students looked at each other as if to say, "What is Kurdish? I've never heard this before," or, "what did she say?" To win or not to win was not the point! I was just thankful I had a loving aunt to help me out.

THE GATHERING CONTINUES

Menashe, Albert, and Jacob went to my Aunt Habiba's villa in Ramat-Gan once a week on Saturday Night. Other visitors were Meir's brothers, Mrad and Joseph who came from Tel-Aviv. Some of the family teenagers, including myself, gathered to talk. Menashe would play backgammon with Meir, his son in law, as he used to do in Baghdad. Everybody was happy to see the old habits continuing despite the messy beginning in the tents of the Ma'bara, A meal would be served and Aunt Habiba would give the kids candies and chocolates as she had in Baghdad.

These happy days did not last long. Menashe stopped coming to Ramat-Gan, the teenagers slowly drifted away, and then we heard terrible news that Aunt Habiba had cancer, which was advancing fast. These happy days did not last long. Menashe stopped coming to Ramat-Gan, the teenagers slowly drifted away, and then we heard terrible news that Aunt Habiba had cancer, which was advancing fast. Her son, Naim, told us that his father was crying everyday, asking G-d not to let her die before him. One day, we heard that Meir collapsed at his home son, Naim, told us that his father was crying everyday, asking G-d not to let her die before him. One day, we heard that Meir collapsed at his home. He had a stroke. Uncles Jacob and Isaac rushed to his house, and the next day he died. The family went to Shivaa every day. One day, after the prayers, she said that she had a dream that Meir needed her, and that he wanted her to join him. Habiba died soon after the Shivaa.

THE FIRST TORAH COVER, IN ISRAEL

For the blessed soul of Mordechai Menashe Mordechai, who past away in April 4, 1951 at the age of 51

Following the fire in the warehouse in Jaffa, Menashe needed a synagogue to house the Scrolls. For two years the Scrolls wandered in different locations in Herzlia, when finally Menashe decided to establish a Sephardic Synagogue and named it Mikdash Melech. The scrolls finally had a home.

Mikdash Melech was a shack, decorated by Rabbi Ezra's precious Scrolls. Abi donated the cover, which is called Parochet, in memory of his son Mordechai. Jacob and Isaac were put in charge of operations and security.

The Torah Scrolls blessed Mikdash Melech Synagogue. It gradually expanded and became one of the biggest Sephardic synagogues in Herzlia and its surroundings.

The two scrolls resided in Herzlia for sixty years. Sixty wonderful years of excitement and heartbeats whenever Hakham Ezra's name was mentioned. Sixty wonderful years of pride and gratitude to grandfather Menashe (Abi) for bringing the Scrolls to Israel. Sixty years of blessings from G-d for saving the Torahs and allowing the next generation to learn about our brilliant past.

The Scrolls were randomly visited and photographed by members of the Murad family living in the U.S., Canada, and the UK. The Scrolls reminded them of their history, of their marvelous past, which intertwined with the life of Hakham Ezra in a time that would never come alive again.

The Mitzvah of Helping Another Synagogue

Ora Rejuan, Rabbi Ezra's great granddaughter, established a synagogue in Tsfat to benefit area residents. She wanted to give those residents a Mitzva of daily prayers, and to guide them into G-d's path of great deeds. She needed to borrow the Scrolls from their current location in Mikdash Melech Herzlia, for a temporary use

Ora Rejuan and Orit Murad Rehany at the Torah Scroll celebration in Jerusalem

in her synagogue in Tsfat. Ora gladly received the permission from Uncle Isaac Murad to use the scrolls. Ora and Rabbi Uriel respected the Torah Scrolls with a great Hachnassat Sefer Torah event at their synagogue. Her synagogue would definitely be blessed to grow and flourish, just like Mikdash Melech did in Herzlia.

RESTORING THE DAMAGED SCROLL

While the Scrolls were out on loan, it was the appropriate time to think about their future for the next generation. It was decided the Scrolls would be officially transferred by Isaac Murad to Ezra Murad. Likewise, Ezra, appointed his son Enav Murad to be in charge of the Scrolls.

Chahla's Scroll needed restoration. For this purpose, generous donations came from the children of Mordechai and Khatoun-Lulu Murad, now living in Canada, the US, and Israel. The donors names are inscribed on the inside plaque of the cover of the Scrolls. Chahla's Scroll was repaired and upgraded; it received a new cover and a silver plaque. Both Scrolls reside now at Beth Ramchal Synagogue in Jerusalem.

The donors names are: Meir and Flora Murad Haviv, Aaron and Tiqva Murad, Emile and Batia Murad, Ezra and Ola z"l Murad, Orit Murad and Saul Rehany.

PREPARATIONS BEFORE THE HSACHNASAH

No one could have ever imagined that the Hsachnasah of Rabbi Ezra's Scrolls would ever take place. The excitement and positive energy encompassed the whole family living in different parts of the world. We are all in awe to the impact Rabbi Ezra left behind, his dear memory, faith and integrity. The idea started less than a year before the set date for the Hachnasah, which transpired in Jerusalem, March 19, 2011.

The excitement took off and increased by the day. Who was going to Jerusalem? Who bought the ticket already? Where did you book your hotel? Is it a hotel or an apartment? Is it safe to rent a car in Israel? And the eternal question of what to wear! The dinner was-debated, the music was handpicked, the speeches were written, and of course there was an outpouring of more donations. From those handouts a booklet was created that told the life of Rabbi Ezra. After intense writing and researching, the booklet was sold by Orit for $20 a copy, with all proceeds donated to Beth Ramchal Synagogue by Aaron Murad.

Invitations were sent out worldwide to all family members. The meaning, the memory, the music, and the speeches, the gathering--everything was fabulous. It was one of the most incredible celebrations of our family to date!

Despite these tragedies, life in Israel amazed me! How instantly I fell in love with this land, my land, my heritage, and the land that I inherited from my ancestors. I was gleeful that I accomplished the ideal of "Next Year in Jerusalem."

THE COURSE OF THE DIFFERENT IMMIGRATION TO PALESTINE

Jews have always desired to live in their homeland to escape Nazism, Anti-Semitism and pogroms.

The rise of the Zionist movement, in the past 150 years the dream of establishing a homeland in the land of their ancestors, became a reality. Here are some of the first settlements and immigrations to Palestine.

Israel today continues to absorb immigrants.

Religious immigration to the Holy Land has always played an ultimate role throughout the years. There were always great Rabbis who immigrated to Holy Land to build a religious settelments.

The Zionists, who are interested to build the land, were the other groups that immigrated to Israel.

The First Aliyah, was in 1882 from Eastern Europe, after facing pogroms and Anti-Semitism. An estimated number of 25,000-35,000 Jews immigrated to Palestine during that time.

The Second Aliyah was during 1904-1914 from Russia estimated 40,000 the majority emigrated United States or South America, a smaller amount joined the First Aliya . These were idealistic immigrants that were ready to accomplish the dream of national renaissance.

The Third Aliyah was a wave of Zionists immigrants from Europe between 1919-1923 from the end of WWI until the start of the economic crisis in the country.

In 1951we had joined them all; leaving the home we had known for generations to establish life in Israel.

The Aliya (immigration) of the Jews from Iraq is known by the name of "Ezra and Nehemiah."

TEL-MOND

The pioneer Lord Melchett, a former British minister and president of the British Zionist Federation, established Tel-Mond. In 1933 a group of famers established Moshav Tel-Mond, and three years later another group established Moshav Kfar Ziv. In 1943 a new group from Yemen established Shechunat Yaacov. In 1950 Neve Oved and Hada Hayim were established to accommodate the large wave of immigration. In 1954 all of these communities merged to form the local Council of Tel-Mond.

In this village, Menashe settled with his son Albert and his wife Louise. Being far from the big city, the place remained undeveloped for a long time. Just a few Egged (busses) traveled there daily at fixed hours. When Ephraim visited Israel from New Jersey in 1952, he was surprised to see his father living in Tel-Mond, far away from Ramat-Gan and Tel-Aviv, where most of his friends and relatives lived. Yet, Menashe never complained, and the respected businessman from Baghdad became a farmer in Israel raising chicken, tending the farm and looking after his garden, surrounded by many trees.

Menashe certainly lived the saying: "Do the best you can under any circumstances, adjust and move forward." Menashe lived through abundance and tragedies; he became a refugee and a farmer with no complaints.

ON THE BICYCLE TO TEL-MOND

One day Jacob and Isaac decided to take bicycles to visit their father in Tel-Mond. The roads were winding, single lanes not much used. One had to avoid an oncoming car by moving somewhat to the right. Once in a while, there was an inter-urban bus (Egged) driving through the areas, and once in a while, a few cars whizzed past.

Jacob brought his son, Menash, and his two daughters Rachel and Ora. All three of them rode on his bike, while Isaac took another three, his son Menashe (named after Abi), and two daughters, Rachel and Aliza. Eight people rode on two bikes from Herzlia to Tel-Mond!!

The ride was exciting and went through the winding roads and under huge eucalyptus trees, and the sun shone high. It was a surprise visit for Abi, Uncle Albert and his wife Louise, but they welcomed family reunion. Unfortunately, it would be the last visit to see Abi.

Eli Murad, Jacob's son and Menashe's grandson, was present at Abi's last moments, and he describes the sad event as follows: "That day I was supposed to pick up Grandpa Abi, and drive him to his house in Tel-Mond. When I arrived, my father Jacob and Uncle Isaac came to the door. They looked worried and anxious. Then we all went to the room, where Abi was: They both knew what was happening. As I entered the room, I saw Abi sitting straight. He asked me for a glass of water. I brought the water. He blessed the water and had a sip. Five minutes later, he passed away, leaving a rich legacy of a righteous honest man."

Menashe passed away at his son's house in Herzlia in 1965 at the age of 90. His life was that of health, riches, and respect.

ISRAEL'S BLESSINGS

Israel's seas and sand, trees and mountains-- its magnificent scenery. One language, one people, and one land, but different traditions and customs that we have to work hard on unifying. We came with one purpose: to help build our land, and to blend and integrate in spite of difficulties. It was a long process of breaking away from rooted ways of previous lives and adapting to the new challenges. The Murad family, and the Iraqi Community, has prospered and thrived in our new land, and we are happy we found our home.

BEAUTIFUL ISRAELI SCENERY

Saul Rehany overlooking beautiful Medeteranian Sea

Wonderful Sachne scenery. Saul Rehany and his life-long friends since their childhood in Baghdad. Left to right: Reuven Yehuda Z"L, Albert Ziv, Yigal Ziv, Eli Benjamin

Rare Trees

Rare Trees

Ramat-Gan known for its magnificent parks

Ramat-Gan's Beautiful Gardens Orit
Murad and Esther Haviv

Enjoy the Photos From the Exciting Evening of the Torah Scroll Celebration in Jerusalem at Beth Haramchal Synagogue

The great Rabbis from Beth Haramchal Synagogue

Mordechai Murad and Mordechai Haviv
both named after their grandfather
Mordechai Murad

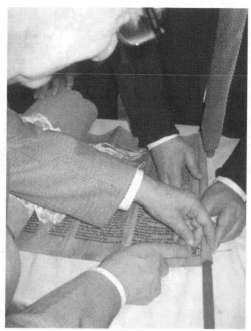

Sticking the Hebrew letters in on the Torah Scroll, raised the excitement to high levels contributing more donations

Guila Matarasso, Saul Rehany and Orit Murad Rehany and Elyiahu

At the Hachnasah in Jerusalem from right: Guila Rehany with Orit Murad and Saul Rehany

Mordechai Murad at the celebration in Jerusalem

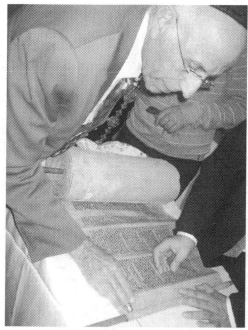

Saul Rehany put letters on the Scrolls

Rabbi Ezra's Torah Scroll. Even after 115 years the scroll looks clear and fabulous

Flora (Fifi)'s children. Left to right: Menashe Haviv, Raya Nachimzon, Esther Haviv Nachimzon

From left: Evelyn Elias Bechor, Orit Murad Rehany, Amanda Elias, Ezra Elias, Aaron Murad Tiqvas Murad, Saul Rehany, Moran Haviv, Lili Haviv Hazmah, Mordechai Haviv

From Left: Ezra Murad, Abraham Kashi, Edmond Itzhaik, Aaron Murad Moran Haviv Tiqva Murad, Saul Rehany

From left: Abraham Kashi, Edmond Itzhaik, Aaron & Tiqva Murad, Saul Rehany

From right: Rinat Murad, Moran Haviv, Esther Haviv Nachimzon, Tiqva Murad Orit Murad Rehany

Our wonderful girls Left to right: Raya Nachimzon, Reny Murad, Moran Haviv, Guila Rehany Matarasso

Chahla's Torah Scroll at Beth Haramchal Synagogue in Jerusalem

Mother, daughter

*Great friends!! Amira Benjamins and Guila Rehany Matarasso.
Background: Samantha Elias from England (Ezra's Elias daughter) is our
family professional writer*

*Beaming with high energy surrounding the room after receiving small
Torah Scroll as a token for our donations. Orit Murad, Aaron Murad
in the background, and the wonderful Rabbis from Beth Haramchal
Synagogue in Jerusalem*

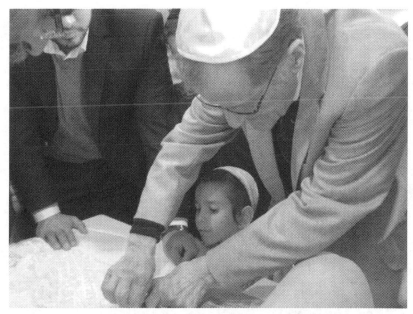

Aaron Murad puts on the Herbrew letters in Rabbi Ezra's Scroll

Orit, Amira and Evelyn Bechor

Conclusion

We hope you have enjoyed reading the rich heritage and legacy of the Murad family. We strived to give an accurate re-telling of our journey from Iraq to Israel, and we researched relentlessly to provide an accurate overview of this unique portion of Jewish history. Our genealogy is compelling and relatable, and we encourage you to share our stories with your loved ones, as we feel it is important to preserve our tales for the future.

Having someone to love is

Family

You can reach Orit Murad Rehany at
Www.OritMuradRehany.com
954-254-2887
orit.rehany@gmail.com